SEXUAL SIGNATURES

Books by John Money

Sex Errors of the Body: Dilemmas, Education and Counseling

Man & Woman Boy & Girl: The Differentiation and Dimorphism of Gender Identity from Conception to Maturity (with Anke Ehrhardt)

The Psychologic Study of Man

A Standardized Road-Map of Direction Sense (with D. Alexander and H. T. Walker, Jr.)

Sexual Signatures: On Being a Man or a Woman

SEXUAL SIGNATURES

On Being
a Man or a Woman

JOHN MONEY
PATRICIA TUCKER

Little, Brown and Company
Boston—Toronto

FIRST EDITION

T04/75

The authors are grateful to William Morrow and Company,
Inc., for permission to reprint excerpts from Margaret Mead's
Male and Female, copyright 1949, © 1967 by Margaret Mead;
and to John T. Early, III, for permission to quote from his paper
"The Sexual Thoughts of a Post-Adolescent."

LIBRARY OF CONGRESS CATALOGING IN PUBLICATION DATA
Money, John.
    Sexual signatures.
    Bibliography: p.
    Includes index.
    1. Sex role. 2. Sex—Cause and determination.
3. Sexual deviation. I. Tucker, Patricia,
joint author. II. Title.
BF692.M582   155.3'3   74-26632
ISBN 0-316-57826-6

Designed by Susan Windheim

*Published simultaneously in Canada
by Little, Brown & Company (Canada) Limited*
PRINTED IN THE UNITED STATES OF AMERICA

Contents

SEXUAL SIGNATURES

1. Orientation

WHEN YOU READ about a grown man who has become a woman do you wonder if you yourself are a man or a woman? Of course not. You knew that you were a boy, or that you were a girl, long before you learned to read. And unless you are one of the very few exceptions to an all but universal rule, you've never seriously questioned it since — however passionately you may, on occasion, have wished you were the other. If there's anything that seems an immutable fact, an eternal verity, in your life it is your sex.

But when you see in person, or perhaps on television, a normal-seeming, attractive woman, and learn that she grew up as a boy, made a good professional and military record as a man, married a woman and fathered children before becoming a woman, what do you make of it? You might ask yourself some such questions as: Is she *really* a woman, or is she *really* still a man? What does "really" mean? Can hormone therapy, genital surgery, dress and makeup turn a man into a woman, or a woman into a man? It wouldn't for me, so how can this person be a woman? But if she is really a man, what is there of her that is a man? What, in fact, does it *mean* to be a man or a woman?

The chances are that after a moment or two of such musing your mind turns back to your own concerns. After all, your life is complicated enough just being what you are, and the dramatic dilemmas of a transexual are not your problem. The question of what it means to be a man or to be a woman, however, is very much a part of your life, for when you come down to it, what are your concerns?

Are you falling in or out of love? Do you wonder if your love life and your friendships ought to be more rewarding? Do you suspect you may be missing something by not sleeping around — or *by* sleeping around? Do you know what attitude to take with your toddler, your teenager — or yourself — about masturbating? Are you uneasy because your small son likes dolls or won't stick up for himself, or your small daughter doesn't and will? Are you expecting a child and do you hope it will be a boy, or that it will be a girl? Are you dubious about sex education courses, or afraid that a homosexual teacher will corrupt your child? Do long-haired boys and male-clad girls affront you? Does a fleeting homosexual or incestuous impulse you once felt haunt you as a possible warning of latent perversion? Are you distressed because your teenager wants to live in a commune, or room with his girl-friend or her boyfriend? Do you fret lest "unisex" take the joy out of gender? Does your wife's paycheck make you uncomfortable, or your husband's or boss's male chauvinism get you down? Are you curious about "swinging"? Does the thought of menopause make you cringe, and do you dread a sexless old age?

Such everyday concerns are rooted in the question of what it means to be a man or a woman. However far they may seem from the medical problems of transexualism, it is from the efforts of scientists to help transexuals and others of ambiguous sex that answers for the rest of us are beginning to come.

Those answers are important to you because your sense of yourself as you, a unique individual — your identity — is the essence of you, and at the core of it lies your sense of yourself as male or female, your gender identity. It is the kingpin of your identity, the anchor of your emotional health. It is there in your love and hate, your work and play, and in all your relationships with others. Your gender identity puts its mark on everything you think and feel, do and say. Your understanding of yourself and others is limited by your understanding of what it means — to you and to them — to be a man or a woman.

This book is a road map to show you where you are now as a man or a woman and how you got there. It can help you keep your bearings in relation to your contemporaries, your parents, your spouse, your children, your grandchildren, society, and yourself, and help you steer a steady course through the storms that lie ahead. Some of the map's features are familiar, many have only recently been discovered, and vast areas remain uncharted, for although sex has been enthusiastically researched by almost everyone who ever lived, the truly scientific investigation of sex differences has only just begun.

The easy assumption has been that there are two quite separate roads, one leading from XY chromosomes at conception to manhood, the other from XX chromosomes at conception to womanhood. But there have always been puzzling exceptions — hermaphrodites, transvestites, transexuals, and homosexuals — to raise troublesome questions, and in helping those people to fit comfortably into one sex or the other, scientists are uncovering a different picture. The fact is that there are not two roads, but one road with a number of forks where each of us turns in either the male or the female direction. You became male or female by stages. Most of us turn smoothly in the same direction at each fork. If it weren't for those who have taken an incompatible turn somewhere along the line, the forks might never have been mapped.

Such a map is needed now as it was never needed before because radical changes in the cultural definition of what it means to be a man or a woman are disrupting our lives. It's true that different societies have had different definitions, and that even in the same society the definition has been different in different eras, but today the *rate* of change has so accelerated that it is fearfully hard for men and women to find common ground. In sex, future shock is no longer future, it is now.

There are those who regard the current disruption of relations between the sexes as a passing storm exaggerated out of all proportion by thrill-seeking youngsters, misfits, and libertines. There have always been two sexes, these people point out, and every society's definition of the behavior appropriate to each has bred gusts of oratory

6

and showers of tears that the human race has always weathered. Those who cling to such views had better take another reading. There are irresistible forces behind the present turmoil, forces that are new in the long history of humanity.

Item: "Be fruitful and multiply," the first commandment of species survival, has suddenly become a formula for human disaster.

Item: For the first time, contraception — the means of separating sex play from reproduction, recreational sex from procreational sex — is available to everybody in the country, male and female, young and old, single and married, poor and rich.

Item: For more than a century the average age of puberty has been dropping at the rate of about a year each generation. The growing spread between earlier attainment of sexual maturity and progressively later attainment of adult social status in our society has transformed adolescence from a brief transition period into a significant stage of life with its own kinds of sexual demands.

Item: Machines that work as well for either men or women do much of the drudgery that has always been assigned by sex.

Item: A century ago "till death us do part" meant to a young bridal couple perhaps twenty years, barely time enough to launch a family; today it can easily mean half a century.

These and more subtle forces are driving us to a radical reassessment of what it means to be a man or a woman. Like it or not, we are living in a sexual revolution and it is changing our lives. We dare not depend on old answers,

7

nor can we afford to cut off the pioneers who are exploring for new ways to meet these unprecedented challenges.

The pioneers of new sexual life-styles see their explorations as attempts to escape hypocrisy, as a search for the integrity without which living is a burden. Conservatives see the pioneering as a threat to integrity, an attack not only on society but on their own sense of themselves as men and women. In all the camps there is the lurking fear that changes in the definition of manhood and womanhood may destroy the precious differences between the sexes, turning us all into either sexless zombies or ambisexual acrobats.

The reason so many people react to sexual pioneering as if it were a personal attack is the constant interaction between individual and society that sustains both. Cultural stereotypes, including the gender stereotypes — society's definition of what it means to be a man or a woman — are the glue that holds a society together. They embody the general agreements that enable a group of people to co-operate. Without a language stereotype, for example, a general agreement on the meaning assigned to a vast number of combinations of sounds, there could be no common language. Gender stereotypes embody the general agreement on the roles assigned to men and women, boys and girls. They are the matrix within which your own personal concepts of what it means to be a person who is a man or a woman — your gender schemas — took shape. Wherever your schema fits into the stereotype, you gain support from society for your sense of identity, and by the same token a change in the stereotype jars your sense of yourself. The severity of the jolt depends on how rigid your schemas are. Like your backbone, they must be rigid enough to support you, but flexible enough so that you can maneuver. The best trade-off between rigidity and flexibility depends on what you want to do, how much support you need, and what kinds of jolts you must absorb.

Your gender schemas are the framework of your gender identity/role. There are very few technical terms in this book, but "gender identity" and "gender role" must be understood. The terms were introduced so recently that not everyone understands them the same way (for a historical account, see Money, 1973a). Gender identity, as described above, is your sense of yourself as male or female. Gender role is everything that expresses this sense of yourself as male or female. Gender role includes everything you feel and think, everything you do and say, that indicates — to yourself as well as to others — that you are male or female. Gender identity and gender role are not two different things; they are different aspects of the same thing, like the proverbial two sides of a coin. Your gender identity is the inward experience of your gender role; your gender role is the expression of your gender identity.* The term "gender identity/role" emphasizes this unity.

While your gender identity/role conforms more or less to the cultural stereotype for your sex, it also reflects the

* Official definitions (Money and Ehrhardt, 1972):
Gender Identity: The sameness, unity, and persistence of one's individuality as male, female, or ambivalent, in greater or lesser degree, especially as it is experienced in self-awareness and behavior; gender identity is the private experience of gender role, and gender role is the public expression of gender identity.
Gender Role: Everything that a person says and does, to indicate to others or to the self the degree that one is either male, or female, or ambivalent; it includes but is not restricted to sexual arousal and response; gender role is the public expression of gender identity, and gender identity is the private experience of gender role.

biographical events of your own life, your body, and your personality, just as the language you use conforms more or less to the cultural language stereotype but also reflects your physical structure, the circumstances under which you learned to talk, where and how you grew up, and your personality. The continual interaction between society and the individual constantly causes some degree of modification on both sides.

Growing up is mainly a matter of shaping up to fit into a society, a vital process since none of us could survive very long as members of no society. If its cultural stereotypes are too rigid, the society stunts its members and stagnation sets in, for rigid stereotypes can maim as severely and as permanently as foot-binding maimed previous generations of Chinese women. But if the stereotypes are too amorphous, the society fails to provide its members with the necessary means of cooperation and soon falls apart. The tendency of cultural stereotypes to resist change is essential for maintaining a society, but flexibility is essential to maintain both the society and its members in health. The societal challenge is to achieve stereotypes that are strong enough to support cooperation but flexible enough to allow for individual development. Those who are outraged by pioneering in new life-styles are reacting on two levels: there's the fear that weakening the stereotypes will cause society to collapse, and the fear that radical change in the stereotypes will leave their own sense of identity without adequate support.

As a starting point for the road map, take the gender stereotypes of our not too distant past. There's no generally accepted definitive description of them, but by and large, the main body of American society accepted, through most of its history, that —

If you are a man:

- You may fight but not cry.
- You must strive to outdo your fellow man, never admitting defeat.
- You may seduce girls to prove your manliness, but are entitled to a virgin bride.
- You may do any work, even the most menial, outside of your home without damage to your pride, but you don't undertake the cooking, cleaning, or laundering at home, or the day-to-day care of your children. (In a domestic emergency you cope, but perform even the simplest domestic chore sloppily to advertise that it is alien to you.)
- You take financial responsibility for supporting the women and children in your immediate family; your wife can perhaps go out to work if she wants to, but her real job is at home.
- You may show affection for your wife and small children, but not for anyone else and most particularly not for another man; if you want to show a man that you love him, you make a mock attack — slap him on the back, shove, or lunge at him.
- All your relations with women are strongly colored by sex, and the significant ones are those limited to sex.
- You brag about the fun and bawdy lustfulness of sex in any all-male group, and use a special prudish vocabulary with women, even your wife and any other sex partner.

If you are a woman:

- You're a failure unless you marry and have children.
- Until you marry, your job is to compete (not too openly) with other women for the attention of men

and to hang onto your hymen, but it's unbecoming to show overt interest in a man until he has signified interest in you.

- After you marry, your job is to be a good wife and mother, and to pay no attention to other men ("good" is defined not in terms of your own performance, but by the well-being of your husband and children or their regard for you).

- Wile and guile are your weapons, manipulation is your tactic; you're not expected to have a strategy or to be consistent, but if your inconsistency — or your children — cause problems, it's your fault.

- You read and write, but not too much of either, and even less of math.

- If you earn a little money, that's great, as long as it doesn't interfere with your homework, but to surpass your husband or his colleagues in any kind of achievement outside of the domestic sphere puts everybody in grave psychological peril.

- Your sexual feelings are not very important; it's not nice to think or talk about them.

Although they've been crumbling for years, these stereotypes have by no means lost their grip. To some Americans, they are still gospel, to others they are quaint, but their influence still reaches deep into the lives of us all.

World War II marked a kind of watershed for gender stereotypes. In the late 1960s, rebellious American youth adopted as a tenet of its credo "You can't trust anybody over thirty." There's nothing magic about the age of thirty, but in the late sixties it had the special significance that anyone who was then over thirty had been born before

World War II. That war severely jolted the gender stereotypes by force-feeding to millions of young men drafted into the armed forces the knowledge that they were not biologically unqualified to cook, clean, and launder for themselves or for others, and taught even more millions of young women that a job and fat paycheck did not make them unfeminine. Rosie the Riveter was a folk heroine, and women who wore uniforms, even those with bars or oak leaves on their shoulders, had no trouble getting dates and wedding rings. The members of that generation had consolidated their concepts of manhood and womanhood long before the war, however, and when peace came and prosperity prevailed, they reverted to the living patterns of their childhood with a rush. The result was an orgy of exaggerated domesticity that produced the phenomenal postwar baby boom. But the shock had jarred loose the glue of gender stereotype, and the children whose basic concepts of manhood and womanhood were formed after that war have grown up with a far more flexible idea of what it is to be a man or a woman. Already there are signs that the children of those children are even less concerned than their parents with arbitrary gender role distinctions, a striking demonstration of progressive interaction between stereotypes and individual schemas.

The accelerating rate of change during the past few decades has made the inevitable gaps between individuals, between the sexes, and between generations so uncomfortably wide that cooperation has suffered. But while the gaps that separate the sexes from each other have been widening, gender research has been finding out more and more about how those gaps opened up and how they can be narrowed. This book examines sex differences in the light of the new findings. It traces your course from the start of your life to show the anatomical turnings that steered you toward manhood or womanhood, the way you put together your concepts of what men and women are, and the interaction of the factors that influenced you at each stage of your sexual development in their historical, cultural, and biographical context. With such a map you can see where you are now and what options are open to both you and society in adapting to the changes that are now taking place.

Much of the new insight into the ancient processes of sexual differentiation is coming from the handful of gender identity clinics now in operation. If you've never heard of a gender identity clinic, you are not alone. It wasn't until 1966 that the first gender identity clinic in the world officially opened its doors at Johns Hopkins Hospital in Baltimore. There, and at a dozen other such clinics that have since been established, specialists in a number of different fields — psychology, psychiatry, sociology, genetics, endocrinology, embryology, and surgery — have teamed up so that the full force of modern science can be brought to bear on sexual differentiation problems and research.

At Johns Hopkins Hospital there are the Gender Identity Clinic, where transexuals and transvestites are treated, and the Psychohormonal Research Unit. Patients seen in the Psychohormonal Research Unit are children with defects of the sex organs and homosexuals, as well as transexuals and transvestites, including those who are being treated in the Gender Identity Clinic.

The labels "transexual," "transvestite," and "homosexual" designate points on the spectrum between stereotypic male and female sexual behavior. They are often lumped together in people's minds, and while it's true that there is some overlap in the areas between the points, you can learn more about normal sexual differentiation by considering them separately.

One source of confusion is that the human mind finds it convenient to perceive by contrast. Bipolar thinking is probably the most primitive form of logical thought, and people talk glibly of light or dark, hot or cold, good or bad, male or female, alive or dead, and so forth, as if there were a sharp dividing line between them. Everybody knows that reality consists of infinite shadings along a spectrum between imagined absolutes, but bipolar thinking is useful, so we use it. The mistake is to forget that the absolutes, if they exist at all, are quite outside human experience, and that any dividing line is largely a matter of context. The same water can be too hot (for bathing) and too cold (for sterilizing); the same illumination can be too light (for sleeping) and too dark (for reading); and shooting somebody can get you jailed or decorated as circumstances determine whether it was a good or a bad act. Just when a person can be pronounced dead is a very serious problem, especially in modern organ-transplant surgery, and one that has not yet been solved. Only the extremes are easy to classify, leaving large fuzzy areas in between.

Abandoning bipolar thinking, you might take dark as a base and think of something — light — being added to it in varying degrees, or you might take light as a base and define dark in terms of decreasing light, and the same for hot and cold. You can think of human nature as grounded in original sin, with something — goodness — added in varying degrees, or you could start with pristine goodness and think of evil as the something that is added.

When it comes to male and female, the Bible tells of

15

Adam as the base with something — a rib — taken away to make Eve. In the light of modern research you might take Eve as the base and think of something — male hormone — added to make Adam, or you could keep Adam as the base with something — again male hormone — decreased to make Eve. We have adopted the Eve base view, and will refer to the something that must be added for male differentiation as the Adam principle. In the sexual differentiation road map, the Adam principle is a recurrent feature, as you will see.

When it comes to sexual behavior, the bipolar fiction of what is masculine and what is feminine posits a purely heterosexual man and woman on one side of the dividing line, and an equally imaginary purely homosexual man and woman — pure transexuals — on the other side. In reality, people are infinitely varied along the spectrum in between, all capable of bisexual behavior. In fact, it is safe to say that every adult human being has, in fantasy, engaged in some form of bisexual behavior, if not physical contact, to some degree at some time in his or her life. "Ambisexual" describes the human race more accurately than "heterosexual," "homosexual," or even "bisexual," although the degree of ambisexuality varies in intensity from one person to the next. With this in mind, we can establish four areas on the gender spectrum to use as reference points on the map of sexual differentiation.

Hermaphrodites

Hermaphrodites, also known as intersexes, are those in whom development of the sex organs took an incompatible turn at one of the forks in the road before birth. How this can happen is described in Chapter 2.

The word "hermaphrodite" comes from the names of Hermes and Aphrodite, the Greek god and goddess of love, whose sacred union was thought to have produced a two-sexed god. Aristotle came close to the actual explanation of hermaphroditism when he guessed that a change in the magnitude of a small organ in the embryo "will turn the embryo from male to female, or conversely, or to neither sex if the organ is obliterated."

Aristotle's successors down to the eighteenth century spun many a fanciful theory of sex determination and hermaphroditism, which have been admirably summarized by Dorothy Price (1972). These might be called old husbands' tales since most of them aimed at placing the male principle on the right side of the body, a trivial but curiously persistent bit of male chauvinism. Galen thought that semen from the right testicle would start a male baby, from the left, a female, and that a mixture of semen from both testicles would produce a hermaphrodite. Avicenna taught that a child's sex depended on which direction, right or left, the penis was pointing at the critical moment of insemination. And so it went until the mid-eighteenth century, when Albrecht von Haller, a Swiss scientist, physician-surgeon, and poet, quashed such theories smartly by proving that a man with only one testicle had sired offspring of both sexes and that a woman with only one uterine tube had given birth to both a son and a daughter. Not even von Haller, however, could figure out how to get a compass reading on a man's penis at exactly the right moment!

When a hermaphrodite is born, the question usually is whether the child is a boy whose testicles have not descended and who has a small, open-guttered penis and incompletely fused scrotum, or a girl with an enlarged clitoris and partially fused labia. Unless someone who understands the problem is available, the infant is arbitrarily assigned to one sex or the other. The result is that there are people who are sexually concordant at birth — born with the same kinds of chromosomes, gonads, hormones, and genitals — some of them labeled male and some female. From the same starting point, some, in consequence, are growing up as boys, some as girls, and of those who are grown, some are men and some are women.

At Johns Hopkins there are files on more than thirty matched pairs — each pair made up of a boy and a girl or a man and a woman of about the same age who were sexually alike at birth. They are not related to each other, they don't know each other, and they didn't come to Johns Hopkins at the same time; they are matched only in the Psychohormonal Research Unit's files. Some have had whatever surgical repair and hormone therapy they needed as boys or as girls from the time they were born; others had to struggle, sometimes for years, to achieve and maintain their gender identity amid conflicting signals from their bodies and from those around them before they got proper medical support. Their successes and problems in conforming to their male or female labels, and the difficulties that confronted them if the label was changed, have told a great deal about when and how a person gets to be a man or a woman (Money, 1968; Money and Ehrhardt, 1972; Money, 1974).

Psychosexual Problems

Homosexuality, transvestism, and transexualism are considered psychosexual because they manifest themselves psychologically and in behavior. So far as anyone knows, they can originate after birth independently of any physiological determinants. The theory that some people are born with a predisposition toward these gender identity disorders may be true, but to date no unusual genetic, hormonal, or anatomical pattern common to any one of these conditions is detectable by laboratory tests that are now available.

Males are considerably more vulnerable to almost every kind of psychosexual nonconformity than females. The ratio of men to women among obligative homosexuals, transvestites, and transexuals is estimated at three or four to one and may well be higher. The paraphilias such as lingerie fetishism, voyeurism, exhibitionism, necrophilia, and the like, are distortions of the male gender identity exclusively. Whatever their immediate cause, they are no doubt indirect manifestations of Adam principle insufficiency. In describing homosexuality, transvestism, and transexuality, we have therefore concentrated on their manifestation in males. It should be understood, however, that the descriptions apply in reverse to females, though it is unlikely that genuine transvestism, in the sense of being dependent on cross-dressing for the achievement of orgasm, occurs in females.

HOMOSEXUALITY: Homosexuality is erotic response to individuals with the same kind of external sexual anatomy as oneself. "Homo" derives from the Greek word

19

meaning "same," not from the similar Latin word meaning "man." Attitudes toward homosexual behavior have see-sawed wildly through the ages. The ancient Greeks considered it as normal as, and entirely consistent with, heterosexual behavior, at least for males. At the other extreme, Leviticus speaks for the ancient Hebrews: "If a man lies with a man as with a woman, both have committed an abomination; they shall be put to death."

The most famous of the ancient homosexuals was Sappho. The word lesbian comes from her birthplace, the island of Lesbos. Sappho wrote hundreds of poems, of which only seven hundred lines have survived. Full of passion and lust, those seven hundred lines contain the oldest avowals of homosexual love we have from the hand of one who felt it; but for all that, Sappho was probably ambisexual rather than homosexual. Some of her love poems were addressed to men, some celebrate marriage. History records that she had a daughter. Most of her surviving lines, however, are offerings to the girls she fell passionately in love with.

In classical times the Romans were quite relaxed about many kinds of sexual behavior, but with the spread of Christianity, Rome defined all sexual activity as sinful, with only a grudging concession to conjugal intercourse for the purpose of procreation. Sex and the human race managed to survive, and so did homosexuality, although the sixth-century Justinian code doomed homosexuals to torture and mutilation as a prelude to the death sentence. Public opinion had relaxed slightly by 1087, when William Rufus, son of William the Conqueror, became king of England; his obvious indications of homosexuality were officially ignored, but still people muttered darkly of "Eastern vices."

Public attitudes toward homosexuality fluctuated between tolerance and revulsion, but in the fourteenth century it was still a very serious charge. When Philip IV of France needed a pretext for appropriating the considerable wealth of the celibate Order of Knights Templars in 1307, he accused the Order of blasphemy and idolatry, and to further inflame the people, he added a charge of sodomy against the entire membership. It worked. The pope disbanded the Order, its members were hunted down to be burned at the stake, and Philip got away with the treasure. His public demonstration of outrage at the Knights Templars' alleged homosexual practices didn't stop Philip from marrying his daughter, Isabella, to Edward II of England, whose lavish gifts of power and privilege to his male favorites eventually led to his deposition. Some of Edward's countrymen, however, expressed their disapproval of his erotic preferences in a fiendish way; the rumor has persisted that Edward II was done to death by red-hot pokers "putte thro the secret place posteriale."

There have been periods all through history when homosexuality was fashionable, but less than a hundred years ago Oscar Wilde was jailed, financially ruined, destroyed as a writer and dramatist at the height of his powers, and hounded to an early death when a court determined he had been guilty of homosexual practices. A similar scandal in Germany a few years later brought disgrace to the kaiser's brother and the suicide of Friedrich Krupp, heir to the Krupp armaments empire.

In the United States today, homosexuals are still routinely dismissed from military and government service and ostracized by much of society if their homosexuality becomes publicly known. A nationwide poll by Indiana

21

University's Institute for Sex Research, reported in the October 1973 issue of *Human Behavior*, showed that two-thirds of the three thousand adults selected as a representative sample considered homosexuality "very obscene and vulgar." A third of them thought homosexuals should be jailed or put on probation, and the majority endorsed job discrimination against them. When University of Maine trustees voted to let the Wilde-Stein Club (named for Oscar Wilde and Gertrude Stein) hold a convention of homosexuals on campus, a tidal wave of reaction swept in. It "made the Vietnam and Kent State furor look like fun and games," University Chancellor Donald McNeil was quoted as saying in the *Washington Post* on May 7, 1974. "For Maine, the homosexual thing went deeper into people's guts." Although it cost the university some state funds and alumni support, McNeil and the trustees stuck to their guns. "It was a stand we had to take — free speech, free thought, human equality — and we took it," McNeil explained.

There are signs that American opinion is beginning to relax. In June 1973, Ann Landers could tell a worried correspondent, right there in her widely syndicated advice column, that "there are very few things in life that are 100 percent anything — and this goes for sexuality. It is entirely normal for a male or a female to have flashes of 'interest' in a member of the same sex." And in 1974, the full membership of the American Psychiatric Association approved by referendum the removal of homosexuality from the association's list of mental disorders.

There are cultures alive and well in the world today that prescribe a period of homosexuality for adolescent males as standard preparation for manhood. The ones that have been studied, including the Batak people of Sumatra

(Money, in Money and Ehrhardt, 1972) and the Marind Amin headhunters of southern New Guinea, appear to be remarkably free of obligatory adult homosexuality. In these cultures heterosexual marriage is universal and couples settle easily into the heterosexual life-style.

One reason the debates about homosexuality usually generate more heat than light is that the debaters are often talking about different points on the spectrum to start with. Furthermore, the debate can shift easily from one point to another without anyone recognizing that the grounds have changed. Before we go any farther, a definition of just what point on the spectrum we're discussing is in order.

As already defined, homosexuality is the erotic response to individuals with the same kind of external sexual anatomy as oneself. It may or may not include overt homosexual behavior and physical contact. Since it's safe to assume that practically everybody has had at least fleeting homosexual fantasies of some kind at some stage of development, we'll eliminate from this discussion all those whose erotic response to members of the same sex confines itself to fantasy and look only at those who actually engage in sexual relations with members of the same sex. This still leaves plenty of variation, for we must distinguish between transient or episodic homosexuality and chronic or obligative homosexuality.

Episodic homosexuals are habitually heterosexual people who engage in homosexual behavior for a limited period or periods. Episodic homosexuality is likely to occur under circumstances that restrict heterosexual opportunities — in prison, prep school, military camps, and on warships, for example. Such episodes are not necessarily repeated later in life. The fantasies of an episodic homosexual may or may not be homosexual. This category also includes those who alternate between male and female sex partners when both are available to them. That kind of behavior is more accurately described as concurrently ambisexual. The slang term AC-DC (borrowed from electricity) correctly indicates that their sexual responses, including their fantasies, can alternate between homosexual and heterosexual.

The label of chronic homosexual extends to normally heterosexual people whose heterosexual opportunities are permanently cut off, as by a life prison sentence, so that if they are to have any sex life at all it must be homosexual. Their fantasies and erotic dreams, which are heterosexual to begin with, may or may not become homosexual.

For our purposes, we will exclude all of the above and concentrate on the portion of the spectrum that covers only obligative homosexuals, those who are capable of responding erotically *only* to other males, in fantasy and usually in fact. Within even these narrow limits there is still another distinction to be made, between those who prefer to take a more masculine role and those who prefer a more feminine role in lovemaking. There are also those who can take either role. A masculine-type homosexual man may be almost indistinguishable from a heterosexual man except for the focus of his erotic interest. In his workaday behavior, he usually differs little from other men and he may even have sexual relations with women, but his affections and erotic interests are directed chiefly toward males. The truly effeminate homosexual, however, differs from the average man in various other ways as well as in his erotic preferences. Like a woman, he enjoys receiving a man's penis, and he may exhibit feminine responses and behavior in other contexts besides that of sex. On the effeminate side, this portion of the homo-sexual spectrum merges into transexualism.

TRANSVESTISM: Transvestism is compulsive cross-dressing and impersonation of the opposite sex. Children normally enjoy dressing up on occasion to play-act and try out the other gender as a game, and many cultures include an annual carnival time when cross-dressing is a standard part of the ritual. Aren't transvestites merely people who carry the game a little farther? No, they are not. Even as small children, there's a compulsion about the cross-dress-ing of a transvestite that distinguishes it from the play-acting of other children.

Transvestism has seldom been considered harmless. The Old Testament commands that if men dress in women's clothes, "their blood shall be upon them." The notorious Roman emperor Caligula appeared frequently in women's garb. He got away with it, for though bizarre, cross-dressing was at least not vicious as were so many of his other eccentricities. King James I of England often put on women's clothes It didn't cost him his throne, but it did arouse his subjects' disrespect. "Rex Elizabeth fuit, nunc Jacobus regina est" ("Elizabeth was king, now James is queen") is one of the more polite witticisms that cir-culated during his reign.

Edward Hyde, Lord Cornbury, governor of New York and New Jersey during most of Queen Anne's reign, as-tonished the colonists by frequently appearing in public in hoopskirt and feminine headdress, toying with a fan. In one of the two known portraits of this viscount who later became the third earl of Clarendon he is dressed like a great lady of his day.

"Eonism" is a synonym for transvestism introduced by

Edward Hyde, Lord Cornbury, colonial governor of New York and New Jersey, impersonating a woman. He was a transvestite who often displayed himself publicly in female guise. Courtesy of the New-York Historical Society, New York City.

Havelock Ellis, who derived it from the name of a colorful eighteenth-century Burgundian noble, the Chevalier D'Eon, whose life has been well documented in a biography by Edna Nixon (1965). D'Eon was a bona fide scholar and a formidable swordsman whose sex kept the courts of Europe buzzing for years. An able diplomat, he represented the French king at the courts of St. Petersburg, St. James's, and Vienna, and also served Louis XV effectively as a secret agent. The year before he was appointed first secretary of the French embassy in Russia, D'Eon went to St. Petersburg disguised as his own (nonexistent) sister, Lia. D'Eon was always popular with both men and women, and "Lia" became a favorite at the court of the Empress Elizabeth. There he shared a bedroom in the palace with one of the empress's ladies-in-waiting for some months without ever blowing his cover. When he went back to Russia the following year in his official capacity, no one seems to have suspected that he and Lia were the same person.

Eventually, however, rumors of his daring adventure leaked out, and, notwithstanding the military exploits that won him the coveted Star of Saint Louis, caused speculation about his true sex, so that when he went to England as Louis's minister plenipotentiary to open negotiations for the Peace of Paris, his political enemies spread the word that he was really a woman. The question so intrigued the public that huge sums were wagered on it on both sides of the English Channel. Although he was offered a fortune in bribes if he would submit to a medical examination to settle the bets, D'Eon steadfastly refused. In defense of his honor and his privacy, he published a general challenge, offering to duel any and all who were impertinent enough to speculate on his sex. In an un-

27

guarded moment, however, he did once declare himself to be a woman. He quickly retracted his statement, and Lloyd's of London, which had insured many of the wagers, refused to pay out on the basis of that one declaration.

When Louis XVI succeeded Louis XV, he inherited problems enough, besides the one of D'Eon. The new king felt little obligation to the doughty *chevalier* for loyal services rendered to his predecessor, and was reluctant to pay the money the Crown owed D'Eon for them, especially since D'Eon, who had spent freely of his own money in accomplishing his missions and had gone heavily into debt, was demanding a large sum. Louis also had good reason to fear that high-ranking nobles who had insulted the *chevalier* would be skewered in duels when D'Eon, the master swordsman, came home from England. The king found a way out of these embarrassments by issuing a royal order that D'Eon "leave off the dragoon's uniform which she is wearing, and to dress according to her sex."

D'Eon returned, and since his pension depended on it, strove to comply with the king's order. Queen Marie Antoinette tried to help by recommending her own dressmaker and hairdresser, and even sending money to pay them. Although La Chevalière D'Eon was as popular as the *chevalier* had been, D'Eon could not be easy in the new role for long at a time, and on one occasion was thrown into the king's prison for appearing publicly as a man. Growing more and more depressed, D'Eon eventually retreated to England, where King George III and Queen Charlotte, who had known and liked the *chevalier*, made the *chevalière* welcome unofficially. The French Revolution cut off D'Eon's pension, however, and he fell ever deeper into debt. He found he could make a living of sorts by exhibition fencing matches in London and the provinces, and although hampered by age and by the skirts which he continued to wear, he could still outfence challengers young and old when he was seventy. A wound, illness, and old age finally ended this career, and his last fifteen years were spent in poverty and loneliness. When he died in London in 1810, an autopsy, verified by a number of people including a doctor, a French count, and an English earl, finally settled the wagers by establishing that D'Eon had the body of a normal male. This came as a great surprise, not only to the public, but also to the woman whose house he had shared during his last fifteen years, and to the physician who had been attending him before he died.

Those familiar with transvestism will understand why D'Eon would never settle the question of his sex during his lifetime, badly as he needed the money he could have gained by it. He simply could not bring himself to renounce irrevocably either his male or female personality. His history indicates that his male personality, dominant until middle age, gradually gave way to his female personality, but neither could completely eliminate the other.

What today's gender identity clinics are discovering is that a genuine, true-to-type transvestite has this kind of two-part gender identity, a sort of Dr. Jekyll and Miss Hyde alternation, each with its own name and personality, and with the clothes, voice, gait, and mannerisms to match. How convincing Miss Hyde is depends largely on how often she has been able to emerge, since no one, not even a normal person, can perfect a gender role, even his or her own, without feedback from others who accept him or her in that role.

The typical transvestite is a man whose behavior when he is dressed as a man appears to be quite normal except for the overpowering urge to dress in women's clothes and take on his feminine personality from time to time. Quite often he is not homosexual, preferring a woman as a sex partner. He changes his gender identity when he changes his clothes, but unlike a transexual, he does not want to give up his penis. C. V. (for Charles Virginia) Prince, a well-known transvestite and publisher of *Transvestia* magazine, states flatly that "a transvestite is always aware of his maleness," that is, of having a penis. Robert Stoller, the psychiatrist who founded the Gender Identity Clinic at the University of California at Los Angeles, considers transvestism to be the way a man who is obsessed with strong feminine desires protects some part of his sense of maleness.

Stoller and others are convinced that transvestism originates in conflicting parental demands on the young child. Hugo Beigel, a psychologist who has worked with transvestites, told Arno Karlen (1971): "The father says, 'Boys should be sturdy,' and neglects his troubled son. The boy's crucial relationship, then, is with his mother. He sees that girls are closer to mama than he is . . . so the boy thinks girls are better off. One could call transvestism feminine protest."

As he grows up, the typical transvestite finds that, even though he may spurn homosexuals and choose a woman as his sex partner, he cannot shed his transvestism, and he cannot be sexually aroused unless he wears some feminine garment, or at least imagines that he does. He doesn't deny all of his male identity, but he needs the impersonation. If he is deprived of it, tension builds up. A soldier in Vietnam wrote of counting the days, longing not so much to get out of combat as for "the exquisite joy of being able to be Dorothy for the evening, manicuring and painting my nails and feeling that everything I'm wearing is just right." Some lingerie retailers find that their best customers are men, including truck drivers, businessmen, pilots, and stevedores, as well as the frankly effeminate cross-dressers or drag queens. There are now some specialty shops that deal exclusively in women's clothes cut to men's sizes.

Laws against cross-dressing remain widely on the books; although they may be zealously enforced in only a few places such as California and Texas, they accurately reflect public mistrust. To a correspondent who recently wrote that the only way he could relax was to put on a negligee, wig, high heels, and panty hose, Ann Landers publicly advised, "For now fella, I hope you'll stay in the house when you're relaxing. . . . Not everyone is ready for this." A few European countries have recognized the compulsive nature of transvestism to the extent of issuing, on the recommendation of a physician, police permits that protect a cross-dresser from arrest.

TRANSEXUALISM: Like the transvestite, the typical male-to-female transexual has a normal male body. Unlike the transvestite, the complete transexual does not have two gender identities. His gender identity has swung all the way over against his anatomy; he considers himself, in the phrase many transexuals use, a woman trapped in a man's body. James/Jan Morris (1974) put it this way: "I was born with the wrong body, being feminine by gender but male by sex, and I could achieve completeness only when the one was adjusted to the other."

The transexual regards his penis as nature's mistake and wants only to be rid of it. A young transexual offered pathetic proof of this when he tied one end of a string to a doorknob and the other end to his penis, which he tried to pull out like a tooth by slamming the door. Others willingly, even eagerly, undergo painful surgery to get a feminine body. It's a hard route, but there is no other resolution for their problems. Medical science can now give the male-to-female transexual a satisfactorily feminized body, whereas, even with intensive psychotherapy, science has never yet been able to masculinize a transexual male's female gender identity once it has swung all the way over to the feminine side. And although the course of surgery to masculinize a feminine body is even longer, more painful, and promises a far less satisfactory outcome, many female-to-male transexuals are equally determined to undertake it (Benjamin, 1966).

The first medically supervised adult sex-change operation on record was performed on a Danish artist, Einar Wegener, also known as Andreas Sparrer, who in 1930 became Lili Elbe. The first such operation to be widely publicized was performed in Denmark in 1952 on the American ex-GI George Jorgensen, who became Christine Jorgensen, now well known as a lecturer on transexualism. The Jorgensen case made headlines around the world, dramatizing for the public the transexual's dilemma — the fact that transexuality is not a matter of simple caprice or willful social defiance, but an insistent inner prompting of great forcefulness and persistence.

At first the prophets of doom warned that operated transexuals would inevitably become psychotic, but such prophecies have proved wrong. Sex-change operations do not, of course, solve all the psychological problems of transexuals, but only a rare few of the several thousand who have now had the operations have regretted it, and most are happier than they were before. A revealing account of the transformation can be found in *Roberta Cowell's Story*, the autobiography of Roberta Cowell (1954), formerly Robert Cowell, an English fighter pilot in World War II.

"For the first thirty-years of my life," Cowell wrote, "I was Robert Cowell, an aggressive male who had piloted a Spitfire during the war, designed and driven racing cars, married and become the father of two children. Since May 18th, 1951, I have been Roberta Cowell, female. I have become a woman physically, psychologically, glandularly and legally."

Cowell claimed he didn't recognize the feminine part of his two-part gender identity until loneliness following the breakup of his marriage led him into psychotherapy. He sensed that his difficulties involved sex but didn't understand exactly how. He had long noted "certain feminine characteristics" in himself, and knew that homosexuals often took him for one of them, but says positively, "I was never a homosexual."

"The biggest shock to my self-esteem," he wrote, "was my discovery through [psychological] tests that my unconscious mind was predominantly female. The evidence of the tests was far too forthright to be denied. And, as analysis proceeded, it became quite obvious that the feminine side of my nature, which all my life I had known of and severely repressed, was very much more fundamental and deep-rooted than I had supposed." Then came the problem of what to do about it. "In this unhappy time," he wrote, "the two possible solutions seemed to be either continuing with life in the certain knowledge that I was going to go on being desperately unhappy, or putting an

33

end to it all. I envied the insane, who had at least escaped from reality." Then he justified himself: "I was sane and knew that I had to face the facts."

After acknowledging his feminine gender identity and deciding to undergo the surgery that would give him a feminine body, Cowell realized that he needed more than this to make him a woman. There was also the matter of mastering feminine behavior with all its nuances before he could be a woman convincingly and not a freak. Because the feminine side of his nature had been repressed, nothing in Cowell's life had given him practice in behaving like, or interacting with people who treated him as, a woman. It always comes as a surprise to amateur impersonators to find how many functionally irrelevant details are imbedded in the gender stereotypes. The perennially favorite play *Charley's Aunt* makes entertaining capital of the innumerable reflex reactions that have attached themselves to social gender behavior.

During a training period before surgery, Cowell found he could turn his talent for design engineering to fashion design. He started a successful dress business, which gave him excellent opportunities to study how women walk, talk, and react to men, as well as how they dress and wear their clothes. Practice runs dressed as a woman, among people who didn't know him, helped him to feminize his behavior.

During this training period, while he was still appearing as a man, Cowell arranged to meet an author whose work he admired. The author turned out to be a full-bearded, pipe-smoking, very masculine type who expressed a low opinion of women. As Cowell rose to the defense of womankind, the author's attacks grew more vitriolic. Finally, after a prolonged pause, the author dropped this bombshell: "I don't really see why I shouldn't tell you — five years ago *I* was a woman."

With these fields of reference established — cultural gender stereotypes, individual gender schemas, gender identity/role, hermaphroditism, homosexuality, transvestism, and transexualism — we can start at the beginning to trace your course from conception to sexual maturity. Your sexual development is mapped in five stages: prenatal, infancy and early childhood, later childhood, puberty and adolescence, and maturity. The full realization of the unique human potential for manhood and womanhood is surveyed stage by stage, and the section on the final stage, maturity, surveys the various pioneer groups and looks for the most promising ways of reaching the destination.

2.   Prenatal Stages

THOUGH IT IS STILL A MYSTERY how life itself began, a great deal is known about how your particular life began. A ripe egg burst from one of your mother's ovaries, moved along the fallopian tube on that side, and settled in her uterus. On that special occasion your father ejaculated two or three hundred million eager spermatozoa that swam toward the tube in a flood of semen. Only one of all this multitude penetrated the egg, creating the single fertilized cell that was the start of you. The chromosomes of that first cell set the chromosome pattern for every cell in your body from then on. So much is generally agreed, but to what extent that beginning influenced your future sex life is still the subject of furious debate.

Scientific sex research, which got off to a promising

start a century ago, at times has bogged down in an unresolvable and muddle-headed dispute over whether nature or nurture is responsible for the differences between the sexes. Freud gave the nativists their slogan when he said, "Anatomy is destiny." This was popularly taken to mean that very narrow limits were set at conception on how you could feel and think, behave and react, for the rest of your life. "Yard, cod and stones" was the ancient phrase for penis, scrotum and testicles, and plenty of people today, including some biologists and doctors, believe that everything that makes a person masculine or not is written in the tablets of the stones.

The nurturist theory is taken to mean that you became masculine or feminine in attitudes and behavior only after you were born. This theory tends to slide over the anatomical sex differences that are evident in the newborn with scarcely a nod of recognition. Culture and environment, the pure nurturists claim, are all that count.

The true answer is important because, if the nativists are right, there is little you can do about the gender problems of everyday life except wait a few millennia for the imperceptible processes of biological evolution to help humanity adapt to changing circumstances. If the nurturists are right, you can change all the rules tomorrow if you want to.

Neither alone is right, for the truth is that you are the product of continual interaction between your heredity and your environment. The developmental pattern laid down for you in the evolutionary processes that produced the human species has been modified at every point, and especially during the critical phases of your development, including your prenatal life, by your personal past and by the constant interchange between you and the substances,

37

conditions, things, people, and culture that surround you. The interplay of all these variables created the unique individual that is you — and you, in turn, make your contribution to the interplay, modifying your environment and consequently modifying its influence on you.

When it comes down to the biological imperatives that are laid down for all men and women, there are just four: Only a man can impregnate; only a woman can menstruate, gestate, and lactate. All the other sex differences, including differences as closely related to the basic four as breasts and beards, are negotiable, so to speak, depending on where negotiation starts in the life cycle of the individual. Many of the sex differences that are commonly accepted as unalterable givens, as eternal verities, remain negotiable until the day you die; other options close forever at some point along the way. A road map shows which are which and flags the set points. For while the four basic reproductive functions are the only irreducible sex differences, there must be other differences between the sexes to implement them, however they are negotiated and whatever form they take. Other sex differences are essential because the irreducible requirement for the survival of humanity is that men and women cooperate *as* men and women at least well enough to survive, reproduce, and rear a new generation. A man's ability to impregnate and a woman's to menstruate, gestate, and lactate are not, by themselves, an adequate basis for cooperation. Even the elemental act of copulation is not a simple act but an intricate series of reciprocal acts that must be coordinated. To arrive at the point of copulation and then to protect, feed, shelter, and rear the young require cooperation of a high order over a considerable period of time. Gender stereotypes, with all their many more or less arbitrary sex distinctions, provide the framework for that cooperation. They must start from the four basic reproductive functions, but they cannot end there. Achieving even a minimum degree of cooperation depends on some kind of division of labor between the sexes, a sorting of behavior in sex, love, work and play. As long as the four basic reproductive functions are allowed for, however, no *particular* gender stereotype is unalterable. A society has almost unlimited choice of role design or redesign.

"In every known society, mankind has elaborated the biological division of labor into forms often very remotely related to the original biological differences," Margaret Mead wrote in *Male and Female* (1949).

Sometimes one quality has been assigned to one sex, sometimes to the other. Now it is the boys who are thought of as infinitely vulnerable and in need of special cherishing care, now it is the girls. In some societies it is girls for whom parents must collect a dowry or make husband-catching magic, in others the parental worry is over the difficulty of marrying off the boys. Some peoples think of women as too weak to work out of doors, others regard women as the appropriate bearers of heavy burdens "because their heads are stronger than men's." The periodicities of female reproductive functions have appealed to some people as making women the natural sources of magical or religious powers, to others as directly antithetical to those powers. . . . In some cultures women are regarded as sieves through whom the best-guarded secrets will sift, in others it is the men who are the gossips. Whether we deal with small matters or with large, with the frivolities of ornament and cosmetics or the sanctities of man's place in the universe, we find this great variety of ways, often flatly contradictory, in which the roles of the two sexes have been patterned. But we always find the patterning.

39

Beyond the four basic reproductive functions, nothing — *nothing* — of the differences between the sexes is immutably ordained along sex lines. If you were to grade a random sample of men and women in the world on each of the generally accepted sex differences and then plot the results, you would find complete division by sex only on the graph dividing those who can impregnate from those who can menstruate, gestate, and lactate — and even here you just possibly might have some doubt in the case of a hermaphrodite. On the breast development graph, most, but not all, of those on the high side would be women, since breast growth is regulated by the hormone that usually predominates in women. On the muscular strength graph most, but not all, of those on the high side would be men, since brute strength is related to the hormone that usually predominates in men. You would find plenty of overlap on graphs for height, weight, aptitudes, and so on down the line to such arbitrarily assigned differences as who scrubs which floors and other divisions that vary wildly with geography and date, such as which sex paints the face.

By encouraging a particular trait in one sex and repressing it in the other, stereotypes reduce the overlap in a society's graphs considerably, but the fact remains that the only absolutely safe assumption you can make about a family is that a man begot the children and a woman gave birth to them. You would have to hedge any other assumption.

In addition to the overlap, you would find that in muscular strength, breast development, and all the rest of the characteristic sex distinctions, except the basic four, the difference between one normal man and another, and between one normal woman and another, can be, and often is, much greater than the average difference between men and women collectively. It's not hard to find a normal man who is more like the average woman than like the average man on any count except the basic four, or to find a normal woman who is more like the average man than the average woman in this or that respect. In other words, within-group differences, even when it comes to the secondary sex characteristics, may be as great and are often much greater than the between-group differences.

It is well known that at the moment of conception you were a single cell packed with chromosomes, including the sex chromosomes, and that the original chromosomal pattern has since been duplicated in every cell of your body. What is not so well known is that there are no less than four major sex differentiation forks between conception and birth.

To your beginning as a cell, egg and sperm had each contributed 23 chromosomes, each chromosome carrying its hundreds of genes like beads on strings. The sperm's 23 chromosomes paired up with the egg's 23 chromosomes, giving the new cell 23 pairs, or a total of 46 chromosomes. Only one pair determined your genetic sex. Mothers always contribute an X to the sex-regulating pair, so everybody gets at least one X. Fathers contribute either an X or a Y. If an X-carrying sperm won the swimming race, you are a chromosomal female; if a Y won, you are a chromosomal male.

All of this no doubt sounds familiar since the principle has been recognized for many years. The details are gradually being filled in. In 1949, the Canadian anatomists Murray L. Barr and Ewart Bertram, at the University of Western Ontario, recognized that an XX cell always

41

contained a sex chromatin spot (now called the Barr body) and they photographed it. Since an XY cell has no sex chromatin, a laboratory test for the Barr body can identify the chromosomal sex of a single cell. It wasn't until 1956 that the number of chromosomes in a cell was accurately counted, however, and some older textbooks still give the number as 48 instead of 46.

So far as anyone can say now, it's a matter of chance whether the winning sperm brings an X or a Y to the egg, but the odds favor Y. According to miscarriage estimates, there are perhaps as many as 140 XY conceptions for every 100 XX. More of the XY conceptions fail to develop, however, so that the ratio at birth is about 105 boys to 100 girls. (There is also the very small chance that the sperm's or the egg's sex chromosome will get lost, or that the fertilized cell will somehow lose or gain an extra X or Y, as described later in the Prenatal Detours section.)

While a recent survey (Westoff and Rindfuss, 1974) indicates that less than half of American couples would rig the sperm race if they could, a great many prospective parents would still like to choose the sex of their next child, especially some of those who already have several children of the same sex. Although today's theories about predetermining chromosomal sex of human offspring are not as colorful as those of the prescientific past, the chances are good that a choice will soon be feasible. One line of research starts from the hypothesis that the egg is more receptive to one kind of sperm than the other during some specific interval after ovulation. Another line of research assumes the acidity of the uterine environment makes the difference between an X and a Y conception. Even more promising are efforts to separate X and Y sperm in semen from the father and then use artificial insemination techniques to introduce only one kind to the waiting egg. Theoretically it should be possible to find a suitable biochemical agent that would discourage one type of sperm, or to make a condom filter that would block one kind of sperm and pass the other. Ericsson, Langevin and Nishino, according to a report of their work in the January 4, 1974, issue of *Research in Reproduction*, found that when sperm suspended in a medium with a low concentration of albumin were layered on solutions with a higher concentration and allowed to swim freely for an hour, more Y-bearing sperm penetrated into the viscous layer than X-bearing. After repeated separations, 85 percent of the sperm in the more viscous layer were Y-bearing, as judged by the frequency counts of the "firefly" test, that is, the number with a fluorescent Y body. An added advantage of this separation on the basis of motility is that the sperm that managed to cross the gradient appeared to be very healthy; unhealthy sperm apparently could not penetrate into the more viscous medium. Since all of these methods are still in the experimental stage, however, the chromosomal sex of human offspring still depends on the luck of the draw.

From your beginning as a single fertilized cell that multiplied rapidly, your cells soon clustered to form the rudimentary organs of an embryo. Sexually, it was an all-purpose embryo with the growth buds — embryologists call them anlagen — of either male or female organs. First there's a pair of gonads, which can develop into either testicles or ovaries. Then there are two sets of internal genital ducts or tubes. One of these sets of structures, called wolffian after Kaspar Wolff, the eighteenth-century anatomist who identified it, develops into seminal vesicles, prostate gland and the long tubes, one on each side, called the vasa deferentia, for a male. The other structure, called mullerian for the nineteenth-century anatomist, Johannes Müller, develops into a uterus, fallopian tubes, and upper vagina in a female. There is also a tiny, protruding bud of tissue called a genital tubercule, which can adapt itself for either sex, becoming either a penis or a clitoris. Below the genital tubercule is an opening that fuses together in a male, or stays open in a female.

For six weeks after conception, XX and XY embryos proceed along the same neutral road of sex development. At the end of the sixth week there's a fork in the road, one branch leading in the male direction. At that point, the Y chromosomes of a male embryo send a message somehow, nobody yet knows how, to the two gonads, left and right, ordering them to proliferate, develop tubular structures, and become testicles. If you had no Y to divert you, you went on for another six weeks before the primitive, undifferentiated gonads began to develop definitely into ovaries packed with egg cells, enough to last you a lifetime. If you got a second X from your father to go with the one from your mother, the double-X chromosomes steered you onto this female branch.

Although the XX or XY chromosomal pattern you had when you were only one cell is duplicated in every cell of your body even now, the sex chromosomes' influence ended once their sex-determining message was dispatched to your gonads. So far as is known, the sex chromosomes have never again played any direct part in programming your sex life.

When it has differentiated as a testicle, the gonad starts manufacturing sex hormone. Cholesterol, a chemical relative of fat, is the raw material for the sex hormone production line. From cholesterol the testes first synthesize pro-

44

SEXUAL DIFFERENTIATION IN THE HUMAN FETUS

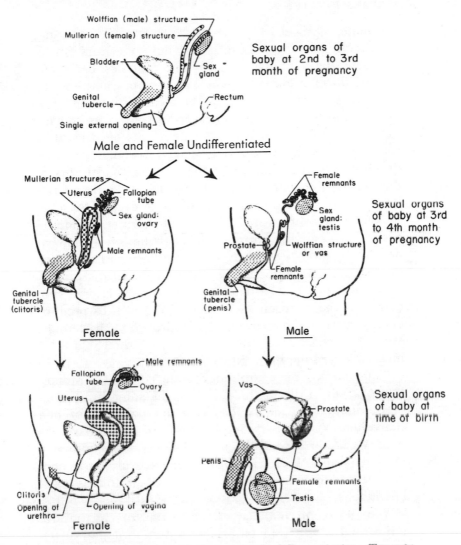

Three stages of normal sex organ differentiation. Top: At second to third month after conception male and female undifferentiated. *Middle:* At third to fourth month after conception male and female differentiation under way. *Bottom:* At birth male and female differentiation complete. Money, Hampson, and Hampson (1955). Courtesy of the *Bulletin of The Johns Hopkins Hospital.*

gesterone, a progestin known as the pregnancy hormone; then androgen, the masculinizing hormone; and finally estrogen, the feminizing hormone. Testicles carry the process through to make some estrogen, but nothing like as much as ovaries produce. Chemically speaking, they are all closely related, but each hormone has its specific functions and each takes various forms. Progestin is called the pregnancy hormone because a woman's progestin level goes up during pregnancy (and also after ovulation during the course of the menstrual cycle in preparation for a possible pregnancy). While androgen is called the male hormone, estrogen the female hormone, and progestin the pregnancy hormone, these names are somewhat misleading since everybody normally keeps all three sex hormones in circulation. The difference is in the proportion of the mixture. Testicles produce enough androgen to dominate the estrogen in a male, while ovaries produce enough estrogen to dominate the androgen in the female. With the sex hormones, it's a question of threshold — of more or less rather than either-or.

The amount of sex hormones produced and the proportion of each in the mixture are not the same in all men or in all women, nor do they stay the same in any one individual. Variation normally stays within limits, however. Variation beyond the normal limits, especially at a critical period of prenatal life, can have dramatic consequences, some of which are described in the next chapter.

Your hormone mix steered you at the fork in the prenatal road where your embryonic internal genital structures, wolffian and mullerian, found their destiny. One set of structures began to develop, the other to wither away. How this happened is a good example of the Adam principle referred to earlier. If you are a man, your testicular hormone production during that critical prenatal period stimulated your wolffian structures to develop as seminal vesicles, prostate, and vasa. The mix also contained a special temporary substance that stopped your mullerian structures in their tracks. If your prenatal hormone mix was not masculine, your mullerian structures went ahead in the normal female way and developed as a uterus, fallopian tubes, and upper vagina, while your wolffian structures began to atrophy. Note that in this second case you didn't need a female hormone mix. Ovarian hormone production appears to be irrelevant to prenatal female sex differentiation. It takes a male hormone mix to make the wolffian structures develop, and it takes that special temporary hormone called simply "mullerian-inhibiting hormone," which is secreted during this period by testicles, to keep the mullerian structures from pursuing their ambition to become a uterus, fallopian tubes, and upper vagina, but it takes no hormonal push at all for this stage of development to proceed in feminine fashion. While the absence of a Y chromosome and the presence of at least two X chromosomes are needed to make a gonad become an ovary, as soon as the gonad fork is passed, the neutral road and the female road converge. Unless there is a sufficient push in the male direction, the fetus will take the female turn at any subsequent fork, whether there is a female push or not. Nature's first choice is to make Eve Everybody has one X chromosome and everybody is surrounded by a mother's estrogens during prenatal life. Although not enough for full development as a fertile female, this gives enough momentum to support female development. Development as a male requires effective propulsion in the male direction at each critical stage.

Unless the required "something more," the Adam principle, is provided in the correct proportions and at the proper times, the individual's subsequent development follows the female pattern.

The Adam principle explains why males are generally more vulnerable to sexual differentiation errors than females. If any one of your sexual systems fail, you can coast down the female road, but not down the male. Population statistics support the general proposition of male vulnerability. As noted above, males lead at conception by something like 140 to 100, but at birth that lead has been whittled down to 105 to 100. While factors other than the Adam principle obviously influence the statistics, nevertheless the trend continues throughout life. The forty-year-old population of the United States is now divided almost evenly between men and women, but in the older age groups women outnumber men, and among those sixty-five and older there are only 70 men left for every 100 women still living.

After your chromosomal sex and your gonadal sex were settled, your hormone mix established, and after one set of your reproductive organs had begun to develop, the other to atrophy, you came to the last fork in the sexual differentiation road before birth, namely, the molding of your external genitals. Here, too, the sex hormones called the turn. "Molding" is the right word because the materials for fashioning either model are the same. Beside the genital tubercule and single opening, the materials are a fold or strip of skin and a small swelling on each side of the opening.

Female molding needs no hormone stimulus, only the absence of male hormone. If your hormone mix was not male, the genital tubercule stayed small to become your clitoris; the two folds of skin did not fuse but stayed separate as the two labia minora and the hood of the clitoris; and the two swellings remained separate as the two labia majora. The opening developed a dividing wall to separate the entrance of the vagina leading to your uterus from the urethra connecting with your bladder.

If your hormone mix was masculine, the genital tubercule became your penis, and the two folds of skin, fusing in a seam on the underside, wrapped themselves around the penis to form a urethral tube. The two swellings fused together and formed a scrotum to receive your testicles when they descended, which they probably did about seven months after you were conceived. The urethral tube connected with your bladder and your prostate gland, vasa deferentia, and testicles. (It is the vasa deferentia that are cut in a vasectomy, an operation that more and more men are electing as a birth control method, for the vasa carry the sperm from the testicles to mix with fluid from the prostate to form semen.)

This last turning point, the molding of your external genitals, got you an M or an F on your birth certifiate.

Prenatal Detours

A map of the prenatal stages of sex differentiation has been built up over the last century or so by studying cases in which development took an inconsistent turn at one of the forks. The possible errors are described here not because they happen very often but for what they tell about how prenatal events interacted with subsequent events to make you a man or a woman.

49

Some people get a deficit of sex chromosomes in that first cell at conception. That means that one X got into place but didn't get paired by either a Y or another X, or that the second member of the X/Y pair was defective. Since it's the second member of the pair that directs the differentiation of the gonads, a single X — often written "XO" but more precisely "45,X" — allows the gonads to remain lazily undeveloped instead of becoming either testicles or ovaries. If the push toward sexual differentiation fails, the individual thereafter takes the female turnings, so an XO always has a female body — because the Adam principle is missing. Lacking ovaries, however, the XO woman will not be able to conceive a child of her own. The ovarian deficit also means that she will need supplementary estrogen at puberty to replace the estrogen that would have been produced at that time by the ovaries in order to bring out secondary sex characteristics such as breast development. It also happens that the missing chromosome prevents her from attaining an adult height of more than five feet.

None of this will keep an XO from developing a feminine gender identity/role. On the contrary, XOs are usually the epitome of conventional femininity. They mother their dolls, adore babies, and take to homecraft like ducks to water. Petite as they usually are, their sturdiness in the face of psychological stress is extraordinary. In short, they are ideal homemakers and mothers of adopted children.

The first reports of people with a surplus of sex chromosomes began appearing in 1959. The most common combinations identified so far are XXX, XXY, and XYY, but there are other possibilities such as XXYY, XXXY, XY/XYY, XXY/XXXY, and several others.

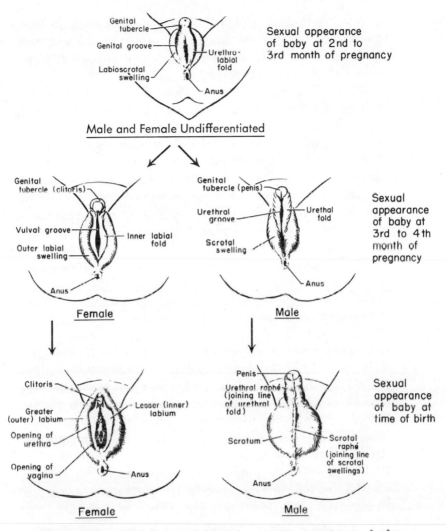

Throughout life a normal male retains vestiges of the structures that could have become a uterus, fallopian tubes, and upper vagina. A normal female retains vestiges of the structures that could have become a prostate gland, vasa deferentia, and seminal vesicles. Money, Hampson, and Hampson (1955). Courtesy of the *Bulletin of The Johns Hopkins Hospital.*

An extra X may not harm a female, and an XXX woman may live a normal life, marry, and bear children without ever discovering that she has an extra chromosome. Some, however, are mentally retarded.

XXY people are male in anatomical appearance, usually tall and gangling. The extra X interferes with normal male testicular development, making the testes sterile. XXY boys and men are more susceptible than most people to behavioral disturbances, which makes it difficult for them to develop adequate personalities. More XXY people have a lower IQ than would be expected by chance, and although their sex drive is weak, a few of them, paradoxically, have gotten into trouble because of antisocial sexual behavior.

The discovery that there are men with an extra Y chromosome was made in 1961. Because the first group of XYY men was identified by a team of researchers whose subjects were inmates of a maximum security prison, the hypothesis was wrongly advanced that the XYY pattern predisposes a man to violent behavior. Further sampling has shown that this hypothesis is too broad. All that can safely be said at this time is that most of the XYYs who have been identified so far are impulsive men, slower than usual in maturing to self-regulation of their behavior. Some XYYs catch up faster than others, and some get into trouble with the law.

With respect to gonads, there are people whose standard XX or XY chromosomes failed to get their message to the gonads properly at the right time of prenatal life. The XY message is garbled more often than the XX message so that it is usually some of the masculinizing instructions that are lost. With incomplete instructions, the gonads of a genetic male cannot differentiate into complete testicles

and cannot thereafter contribute their full quota of androgen to help the individual become masculine. More rarely
it's the XX message that is garbled, perhaps in such a way
that the gonads become neither testicles nor ovaries but
ovotestes, a condition known as "true hermaphroditism."
Even more rarely, an XX message gets so twisted that the
gonads of a person who seems to be chromosomally female actually become testicles, but the full story in such
cases has not yet been deciphered.

An extremely rare hermaphroditic condition is one
called true lateral hermaphroditism, which gives an individual an ovary on one side and a testicle on the other.
How this happens has not yet been adequately explained,
although it has given rise to various myths and legends. As
a rule, the true lateral hermaphrodite has XX chromosomes, but may instead have a mosaic combination of
X/XY or XX/XY. The cells in one part or organ of the
body may have a different chromosomal pattern from
those in other parts of the body, or the mosaic mixture
may be found in all organs.

At the prenatal stage when hormones take a hand in
controlling prenatal sexual differentiation, the chances of
deviation from the norm increase somewhat.

Masculine fetal differentiation is complicated by the
fact that the wolffian structures have to be hormonally
stimulated and the mullerian structures have to be hormonally restrained. If the mullerian-inhibiting hormone
is lacking in an otherwise normal male hormone mix, or
if it fails in its mission, a perfectly good male may find
himself equipped with a perfectly good (although non-
functioning) uterus and fallopian tubes along with the
usual male internal anatomy. The superfluous womb
causes trouble by hampering the descent of the testicles.

53

Since testicles kept inside the body instead of swinging free in the scrotum — where air conditioning lowers their temperature — can't produce live sperm, sterility is the rule for these men, unless the extra organs are removed and the testicles brought down at an early age. Even then, sterility may still ensue.

It can also happen that the body cells of a genetic and gonadal male whose testicles produce ample androgen cannot use the androgen. This condition is known as the "androgen-insensitive syndrome." It is a hereditary defect, transmitted like hemophilia through females but affecting only their genetically male offspring. Unable to heed instructions from the testicular hormones, the wolffian structures of an androgen-insensitive fetus fail to become proper prostate, seminal vesicles, and vasa deferentia. The inhibiting message, however, usually *does* get through to keep the mullerian structures from developing so that the individual ends up with neither male nor female internal genital organs complete. The lower vagina and other external genitals are molded in the female pattern so that at birth the infant looks like an ordinary girl, gets a female label on her birth certificate, and is raised as a girl. There's no reason why she won't live happily unaware of her XY chromosomes as a girl and woman, although at puberty she will wonder why she, in every outward aspect a perfectly normal girl, does not start to menstruate, and later she will find that she cannot get pregnant.

Her XY chromosomes will not keep her from becoming a woman. There is enough estrogen in the testicular hormone mix to give any boy breasts like a pin-up girl's and cause his body fat to deposit in a rounded pattern during adolescence if the estrogen is not dominated by the androgens that direct the emergence of masculine secondary sex characteristics. The undescended testicles of androgen-insensitive youngsters produce ample androgen, but because their body cells cannot respond to the androgen's instructions, these girls continue to look feminine. Their breasts develop, their bodies round out, their voices do not deepen nor their beards start to grow. An androgen-insensitive woman may need minor surgery to lengthen the upper vagina for satisfactory sexual intercourse, but she can fully enjoy her sex life as a normal woman, including orgasm. If her testicles are discovered and surgically removed either early in life or at puberty, she will be given estrogen pills in adolescence and adulthood to take the place of the estrogen the testicles had been supplying, and the result will be the same.

Whether or not the testicles are removed, the outlook for this androgen-insensitive child assigned as a female is good. An example of how good is that of the married couple, a doctor and his wife, who went to a specialist to find out why they hadn't been able to produce children. She obviously knew that something was wrong for she had been faking menstrual periods since adolescence, but neither of them had any suspicion that she was, in fact, chromosomally and gonadally an imperfect male, her body insensitive to androgen, although in all other respects she was normally female.

There is also the possibility of a borderline androgen insensitivity — of body cells that can make only partial use of androgen, so that the child is born with a clitorine penis lacking a urinary tube and only slightly larger than an ordinary clitoris. The testicles can be felt as lumps in the groin. The scrotum is partially unfused. By far the best solution for this child is to be labeled female and raised as a girl, with surgical and hormonal rehabilitation

55

as needed. If this decision is made early in her life and followed through, she can live as happily as the androgen-insensitive doctor's wife. Surgery can feminize the genital appearance by reducing the size of the phallus and separating the scrotum to open the vagina. Removing some of the phallic tissue and deepening the vagina need not interfere with the capacity for orgasm. Orgasm is nature's reproduction insurance, and so intent is nature on maintaining it that surprisingly large amounts of sexual tissue can be removed or relocated without destroying the capacity for orgasm.

Some partially androgen-insensitive infants have unwisely been labeled male and raised as boys, usually because the doctor in attendance didn't fully understand the prognosis, or perhaps because he hesitated to meddle with what he mistakenly regarded as "God's will." Or perhaps the parents, confused by the doctor's uncertainty and influenced by outdated religious precepts, refused to relinquish the prospect of having a hoped-for son no matter what it might cost the child later. For such a baby the outlook is not good. Surgery can complete the fusion of his scrotum and bring his imperfect, sterile testicles down into it, but it cannot make his penis grow. Later his penis may be capable of erection and orgasm, just as a clitoris of the same size is, but it will not be adequate for the male role in sexual intercourse. At the minimum extreme, an erect penis must be something over two and a half inches in length to penetrate far enough into a vagina for a man to begin to feel satisfied with what he can do for his partner. With a short penis, or even after his penis has been amputated, a man can experience arousal, feeling, and climax, but not being able to reciprocate in coitus can inflict terrible wounds on his ego. Surgery can remove the

Those who look like boys at birth, with a clitoris the size of a penis or an actual penis with a penile urethra, and whose labia have fused to become a scrotum, are likely, of course, to be labeled male and raised as boys, even though the scrotum is empty. With adequate help at puberty, such a boy can have a normal male life, except for fertility. If the female status of his internal genitals announces itself at puberty in budding breasts, the onset of menstruation, and the promise of feminine body curves, he will need surgery to remove ovaries and uterus and androgen therapy to masculinize his body. These procedures will keep him looking like a male, deepen his voice, and start his beard growing. His phallus, if not as large as the average penis, will be erectile, and prosthetic testicles made of silicone rubber can be inserted in his scrotum to normalize his genital appearance. Although he will be sterile, he is not more likely to become homosexual in the sense of falling in love with boys and men than if he were an XY with testicles and prostate. In short, despite his XX chromosomes, he can become a man not noticeably different from other men.

As an example, there was the man who first came to Johns Hopkins when he was twenty-four years old. Even with his medical history open on the desk, it is hard for the experienced medical professionals who have followed his case to believe that he was ever anything but a normal male. Nothing in his appearance, manner, gestures, or conversation betrays the fact that genetically and gonadally he was born female. He had looked like a boy at birth, although there were no testicles and the penis was somewhat deformed. He was labeled male and raised as a boy on the assumption that the testicles were there but had not descended. Since his family was quite relaxed about nudity, he had recognized at an early age that he was not as well equipped genitally as his father and brothers, but it never occurred to him to doubt that he was a boy who would become a man and marry a woman. By the age of seven he had singled out a little girl as his sweetheart.

As he approached puberty, his breasts started to develop and his body began to round out. Those who believe that anatomy is destiny would expect these anatomical developments to be reflected in his outlook. On the contrary, he regarded his breasts as a deformity and wanted only one thing of the medical profession — to be rid of them. An exploratory operation at that time revealed ovaries, a uterus, and a vagina that opened internally into the urethra near the neck of the bladder, but no male reproductive system. Even when the boy understood, as he described it, that "they'd found some kind of female apparatus in there by mistake" and that he would never be able to sire offspring, his concept of himself as a male remained unshaken; it never seemed to him that he might "really" be a girl. The female organs were removed, eliminating the menstrual process which had just begun, and he was put on replacement male hormones to stop breast development, distribute his body fat in a masculine pattern, and direct masculine bone growth. His voice soon began to deepen and his beard to grow.

At nineteen this man had a passionate love affair with a girl, and the following year he met and fell in love with the girl he later married. Before they became engaged he told her the facts about himself as he understood them, and they both discussed the situation with his doctor. After he had a minor operation to position his penis more favorably for intercourse, they went ahead and married.

His penis responds readily, and although it is only two inches long when erect, they overcame that handicap so that from the start their sex life was satisfactory to them both. Like many honeymoon couples, they made love daily at first, and in this respect their honeymoon lasted more than six months. Two years after their wedding he reported with dreamy sincerity, "We think we're the luckiest people in the world."

In contrast with this man's history, there is in the Psychohormonal Research Unit the record of a woman who also has XX chromosomes and was born with ovaries and a clitoris resembling a penis. Internally she had a uterus. Before birth she had been androgenized by secretions from her adrenal cortices. She looked sexually ambiguous at birth, but was labeled female and raised as a girl. As she went into an early puberty, however, the secretions of her adrenal cortex managed to gain ascendancy and completely suppress her ovarian hormones. Her body masculinized like the body of a teenage boy. This suggestion that she might be a boy repelled her. Her enlarged and erectile clitoris seemed to her a calamity, and at age twelve she came to Johns Hopkins for treatment.

Fortunately it had been discovered in 1950 that cortisone can be manufactured synthetically, and that it can be used to suppress the androgenizing effect of male hormones. Cortisone therapy allowed this girl's ovaries to take control and feminize her body. Surgery reduced the size of her embarrassingly large clitoris and opened her vagina. The pubertal changes initiated by the androgenizing adrenal secretions had already begun to enlarge her Adam's apple so that her voice was deep. This change could not be reversed, but she learned to use her voice so that she sounded like a husky-voiced girl instead of like a boy. Since then she, too, has grown up and married. So far she has given birth to a son and a daughter, both normal children.

These three people — the doctor's wife, the happy husband, the contented mother — and others like them show that the answer to the question of what makes you a man or a woman is not controlled exclusively by your chromosomes or your hormones, or even by your sex organs themselves. The effects of rearing need to be added, just as they do in order for you to have a native language.

3. Sex Hormones on the Brain

THERE'S ONE MORE STEP in prenatal sex differentiation, a step so newly discovered and so easily mis-
understood that it deserves a chapter by itself, and that is
the influence of prenatal sex hormones on the brain pathways. Only a few years ago researchers would have scoffed
at the suggestion that there could be any such influence,
but today the evidence is unmistakable. The finding that
sex hormones affect the developing brain pathways of
the human fetus is generating shock waves that make it
hard to see in proper perspective. To put the discovery
into perspective, and also because it offers a splendid ex
ample of the way gender research progresses, we'll trace
the history of this discovery before describing it. The pre-

1972 work cited in this chapter was covered by Money and Ehrhardt (1972) and is fully referenced there.

About 1950, Emil Witschi, a Swiss biologist then working in the United States, published reports of his experiments with sex differentiation in frogs. Building on the work of his predecessors, Witschi and his team found that by simply adding female sex hormones to the swimming water of tadpoles, they could make male tadpoles differentiate as female frogs complete with ovaries. What's more, they were fertile females. The sex reversal was so complete that when these genetically male tadpoles matured as frogs they laid eggs that hatched live tadpoles when fertilized by normal male frogs. Witschi could also persuade female tadpoles to develop into fertile male frogs, but for the female-to-male reversal, male hormone in the swimming water was not enough. Testicular tissue taken from male tadpoles had to be grafted into the female tadpoles before they could become males. According to the Adam principle, the "something more" needed to promote male differentiation in this case was male hormone supplied by a testicular graft.

In 1955 in Japan, Toki-O Yamamoto reported parallel findings with killifish. Yamamoto's female hatchlings, however, would obligingly develop as males, and males that could reproduce, without any grafts. Controlling the quantity of male or female sex hormone in the hatchlings' swimming water was all that was needed to permit a killifish sex reversal in either direction.

Then, D. R. Robertson (1972), a University of Queensland zoologist, reported that for the little scavenger fish *Labroides dimidiatus* sex is a political perquisite. These fish, which earn their keep on Australia's Great Barrier Reef by cleaning the mouths and gills of larger fish, travel in small groups. The biggest and strongest member of each group, the leader, is a male; the others are females. If the leader dies, is killed, or wanders off, the biggest and strongest of the females takes over his job — and his sex. Within hours after a leader has left, the new leader starts reconnoitering the group's territorial borders and bullying the other females, and within a fortnight or so begins producing sperm to fertilize the females' eggs. But if a bigger, stronger *L. dimidiatus* happens to swim in and succeeds in challenging the leader for the top job, the deposed leader dutifully retires to the ranks, turns back into a female, and again contributes her share of viable eggs to keep the species going.

Meanwhile, other researchers had picked up the same trail and begun studying sex reversal in mammals, a much more difficult proposition. Female fish and frogs expel their eggs in water for males to come along and fertilize later, which makes it easy for researchers to control the environment of the eggs and to intervene experimentally at any stage, even at the very moment of fertilization. Since the eggs of mammals are fertilized and hatched inside their mothers' bodies, experimental intervention is much more complicated and less precise. Nevertheless, the effect of controlled prenatal doses of sex hormones on the sexual differentiation of opossums, guinea pigs, hamsters, rabbits, mice, and monkeys has been tested and turns out to be far-reaching, although not far enough to make the sex-reversed adults fertile. The experimentally sex-reversed mammals matured either as genetic males with female bodies and female mating behavior patterns, or as genetic females with male bodies and male mating behavior patterns, but they couldn't reproduce.

A very specific difference between males and females throughout the mammalian kingdom is the cyclical nature of female ovarian activity. The cycles are controlled by hormones called gonadotropins (gonad-seeking), which are secreted by the pituitary gland, a gland that nestles deep in the brain behind the bridge of the nose. Regular waves or surges of gonadotropin production bring adult females of subprimate estrous species into heat periodically and control the menstrual cycle in female primates. Gonadotropin production in males is steadier; it may fluctuate, but not in regular, well-defined cycles.

Rat experiments showed that an overdose of androgen (or other related hormones) during a critical period of prenatal life disrupts gonadotropin production. When the female offspring of mother rats were dosed with androgen prenatally or immediately after birth, they were in heat all the time after they matured. The research also showed that the way to induce a regular cyclical pattern of gonadotropin production in adult male rats is not to expose them prenatally to extra estrogen, but to cut down on their supply of androgen during the critical prenatal and immediate postnatal period. When prenatally underandrogenized male rats matured, the pattern of their gonadotropin production was regular and cyclical like that of females, and stayed that way for life. Here the Adam principle turns up again: It takes a push at critical periods to make an individual, male or female, develop in the male direction; whenever the push is lacking or weak, the female pattern establishes itself.

It's worth digressing for a moment to point out some by-products of work along these lines that call urgently for further investigation. In 1970, F. Kobayashi and R. A.

Gorski of the University of California at Los Angeles found that certain drugs can be used experimentally to produce antiandrogenizing effects on rat pups, inhibiting their male differentiation. Among such substances are two of the barbiturates — phenobarbitol and pentobarbitol — which are sometimes used in treating various human conditions, and actinomycin-D and puromycin, which are experimental antibiotics not used on human beings. While it would be premature to conclude that related kinds of substances that might be taken by a pregnant woman, perhaps unknowingly, might have a similar effect on the human fetus, caution and further research are in order.

There is evidence that maternal stress also can interfere with prenatal male differentiation. In 1972, Ingeborg Ward at Villanova University found that when she subjected pregnant rats to extreme stress conditions, their male offspring had shorter penises and testicles of lighter weight than those of rats born to unstressed mothers. When they matured, the experimental male offspring took less readily to male mating behavior and more readily to female copulatory positioning than did normal male rats. Some displayed no sexual interest at all. These findings raise provocative questions about the possible origin of masculine failure in effeminate homosexual men.

Probably more relevant to human problems than fish and rat research is the work on how prenatal sex hormones affect our close relatives, the other primate species. In 1966, Charles Phoenix, Robert Goy, and the late William C. Young of the Oregon Regional Primate Center reported that when they injected monkey mothers with heavy doses of androgen during critical periods of pregnancy, the female offspring were born with normal female reproductive systems inside, but with a penis and empty scrotum outside. What further intrigued the gender researchers at Johns Hopkins was that as youngsters, the monkeys of Goy and Phoenix played more boisterously than normal female monkeys, although their play was not exactly a replica of that of their male peers, and was rather less in frequency. As they matured, their assertiveness and mating behavior, too, fell somewhere in between that of normal male and female monkeys, but rather more toward the male end of the behavior spectrum. Experiments are now under way to find out if prenatal exposure to antiandrogenizing agents will cause male monkeys to look and behave more like females. These experiments are not yet completed, but similar research on rats and hamsters indicates that such an effect must be expected.

Although the other primates are our closest relatives, it's still a far cry from monkey to man, and there are plenty of booby traps for the unwary when it comes to drawing conclusions about people from monkey research. The next step was to find out whether prenatal sex hormone exposure has comparable effects on humans. Since there's no good medical reason for administering experimental sex hormones to pregnant women, the first problem was to find a test group. In fact, there are three such groups, those mentioned in Chapter 2. There are gonadal males whose bodies respond only partially to androgen both before and after birth so that they are underandrogenized all their lives; there are gonadal females whose own adrenal cortices androgenized them before birth and also after birth until the condition was corrected; and there are gonadal females born during the 1950s who were androgenized by the synthetic progestins given their mothers to prevent miscarriage. The girls in this last group are normal except for the prenatal androgenization which came from external sources and ceased at birth. Ten of them were enlisted for the first study at Johns Hopkins (Ehrhardt and Money, 1967) and studies of others have been conducted since and are continuing.

The synthetic progestins did not affect the internal sex organs of any of these girls. The effect on their external genitals ranged from zero through degrees of masculinization that were either negligible or easily corrected by postnatal surgery, to complete masculinization of the clitoris so that it looked at birth like a normal penis, which also had been corrected by surgery. None have needed hormone therapy; since their ovaries were not affected, the girls' own bodies have always produced the normal female hormone mix. Once the androgenization stopped, their bodies developed normally, and all those who have now passed puberty experienced a normal puberty. They don't pretend to be boys, and they don't wish to change sex. In other words, the prenatal androgenization has not been a handicap to them in differentiating a feminine gender identity/role. The differences between the girls in the test group and a control group, made up of girls who were selected to match them as closely as possible except that they had not been prenatally androgenized, can be summed up in the one word "tomboy."

To be a tomboy does not, of course, make a girl abnormal. Many girls go through tomboy periods, and some of the control girls reported tomboy episodes. The difference was that almost all of the test girls were consistently, even boastfully, tomboys throughout childhood. Parents and playmates didn't hesitate to substantiate the test girls' claim to the tomboy title. Interviews and psychological tests filled in the details. The prenatally androgenized girls like strenuous physical activity, cavorting about on their bicycles, climbing trees, hiking, and exploring. They join the boys in rough group games, including football; they like the competitiveness of it. Their dolls may stay on the shelf from Christmas to Christmas, but not their cowboy gear, toy cars and guns. Rather surprisingly, they have kept their dominance toned down below the boys' level, although they are well able to assert themselves. We surmise a double-barreled reason for this mildness. First, they aren't much interested in outrivaling other girls, and second, they sense — or learned early — that boys won't easily tolerate a girl who is too pushy. Perhaps the test girls choose to yield the leadership positions they could win in all-out competition as insurance against being excluded from the boys' games.

Another difference between the test girls and the control girls is in their attitude toward clothes. The test girls aren't rebels. They don't mind dressing up for church or for a visit to grandma, or a party, but they prefer everyday clothing that doesn't restrict them or hamper energetic play. It's not a matter of demanding pants and shirts that were made for boys, and there's nothing compulsive about it. They just don't want to be bothered with fussy clothes. For the test girls it's blue jeans by choice, and skip the frills. In fact, the average of concern for appearance in this group of girls was well below that found in random groups of boys. Some of them, however, like to wear perfume, whatever that may signify.

With regard to plans for the future, the test girls take it for granted that they will eventually marry and have children, but they are less interested in the subject of weddings and babies than the control girls. Their ambitions center on their future careers, both before and after marriage. While most of the test girls prefer boys to girls as playmates (hardly surprising since if you like rough-and-tumble play, you're more likely to find it with boys), most of the test girls center a romantic interest on boys. There's nothing in the histories of any of them to indicate that they are more likely to become lesbians than are any other girls. However, older girls with the adrenogenital syndrome, which has similar effects, have been somewhat slower than control girls of the same age about beginning to date.

To find a parallel group of boys, one doesn't look for prenatally overestrogenized boys for the simple reason that there aren't any. Enough extra estrogen to produce a de-androgenizing effect would, as already noted, almost certainly cause a miscarriage. Since androgen must be added for male development, the counterpart of a prenatally androgenized girl is a prenatally androgen-deficient boy.

Among the prenatally underandrogenized boys are those whose body cells are unable to make full use of androgens, the partially androgen-insensitive boys. Since there is no way to correct this condition, androgen insensitivity continues throughout life. Thus there are no boys exactly comparable to the girls whose overandrogenization stopped when they were born. Nevertheless, the profile of the underandrogenized boy is pretty much the mirror image of the overandrogenized girl. The typical boy in this category is quieter than most boys, less inclined to join in competitive sports himself, though he may be keenly interested in which team wins the pennant. The gender identity of those reared as boys is masculine; they are no more likely to become homosexual than the test girls are to become lesbian.

The "feminine" flavor of such a boy's personality may be less obvious than the tomboy's "masculine" tilt because of the social pressures put on him to disguise it as much as he can. The current feminine stereotype in our culture is flexible enough to let a girl behave "boyishly" if she wants to without bringing her femininity into question, but any boy who exhibits "girlish" behavior is promptly suspected of being queer. There isn't even a word corresponding to "tomboy" to describe such a boy. "Sissy" perhaps comes closest, or "artistic" and "sensitive," but unlike "tomboy," such terms are burdened with unfavorable connotations. This is quite unwarranted, since there is no basic element in the behavior of the underandrogenized boy that is basically incompatible with a masculine gender identity/role.

Since it's a safe prediction that the foregoing prenatal hormonal findings are going to be distorted out of all recognition by nativists, sex chauvinists, and the more emotional sex liberationists, it's essential that the rest of us be very clear about just what it is they show.

Perhaps it will help if we elaborate the road map metaphor a bit by picturing gates at the either-or forks in sexual differentiation. In species like *Labroides dimidiatus*, all the gates stay open so that it's possible for an individual to pass back and forth, able to function fully as either a male or a female throughout its adult life. In frogs and most fish, the gates may stay open for a considerable period but close tight at some point, locking the individual in as male or female both anatomically and behaviorally. In the mammalian kingdom, some of the gates lock earlier, others stay open longer, and as you move up the scale to the primates, the sexual behavior gates gain some independence of the anatomical gates. In the primates, and especially in humans, some of the sexual behavior gates become barriers, solid lines, or broken lines on the development road map, guides to the behavior on one side or the other of a lane, but no longer gates that lock.

As you approached each gated sex-differentiation point, you could have gone in either direction, but as you passed through, the gate locked, fixing the prior period of development as male or female. Your gonads, for example, could have become either testicles or ovaries, but once they became testicles they lost the option of becoming ovaries, or if they became ovaries they could never again become testicles. In behavior, however, at first you drove all over the highway, but as you proceeded you tended to stick more and more to the lanes marked out and socially prescribed for your sex. The lines and barriers dividing male from female for each kind of sex-linked behavior vary according to your culture and experience, and the kind of individual you have become makes a difference in how you feel about crossing them, but you never lose these options entirely. A sufficiently strong stimulus — physical, hormonal, neural, or social — can push you over practically any behavior line or barrier. Your own experience and alterations in the gender stereotypes of your culture can obscure established lines and lower barriers so that crossing becomes easier or harder. For example, a lot of men are wearing their hair long today who only a few years ago would have found it next to impossible to do so.

Anatomical sex differentiation locks some gates so that they can't be reopened. Thus there are a few kinds of behavior which you cannot engage in unless you have a penis and testicles, and a few others you cannot engage in unless you have a vagina, uterus and ovaries, but with these narrowly limited and specific exceptions, there is no kind of behavior appropriate to the human species that is impossible to you because of your sex. Transvestites and transexuals are proof of this, and there is even more dramatic proof when — as occasionally happens in extreme senility or during a rare type of temporal lobe epileptic seizure — a conventionally masculine or feminine person suddenly switches completely over into the other sex role.

The play of infant primates shows the interchangeability of even copulatory behavior. All young monkeys, regardless of sex, play at mounting and at presenting their rear ends to be mounted. Eventually a broken line appears on their road map with the result that male youngsters more often mount, females more often present. Each will carry the preferred behavior pattern further in development as they sort themselves in the lanes of the copulatory behavior they will use as adults, but throughout their entire lives the members of both sexes may cross the rising barrier to engage, in part, in the behavior preferred by the other sex when nudged by circumstances or even just for a lark. Training and experience form ruts that make it more of an effort to change lanes, but the barriers and lines can be crossed. Beyond copulatory behavior, both male and female monkeys engage in strenuous physical activity, jockey for position in the pecking order, and respond to baby monkeys. On the average, however, and under the same conditions, primate males need less prompting to engage in activities that require a high expenditure of physical energy than do females, and they jockey for position more readily and more persistently than females, and the males need more prompting than their sisters to make them attentive to the helpless young. The effect of prenatal overdosing with androgen on the female monkeys is to raise their threshold to parental behavior so that they need somewhat more prompting than other monkey females before they pay attention to monkey babies, and to lower somewhat their threshold to strenuous physical activity and dominance behavior so that they are more eager than other monkey females to romp boisterously and assert themselves.

It's a natural assumption that if your sex makes it easier for you to cross the threshold or barrier into one kind of behavioral lane than another, then you will find it easier to practice that behavior, but the evidence doesn't quite support that assumption. Once the line or barrier is crossed the behavior affected by the prenatal sex hormones doesn't seem to be any more difficult for one sex than for the other. The average differences in proficiency between the sexes can be accounted for easily by the accumulation of experience in the preferred type of behavior. This comes out in a report published in *Science* in 1967. Jay S. Rosenblatt found that an adult male rat would lick helpless newborn rats and retrieve them to the nest no less proficiently than adult female rats do, but it took him longer to start doing it. Mother rats set about caring for newborn pups instantly, virgin female rats procrastinated for a few hours before doing so, and male rats needed about a week of exposure to newborn litters as a stimulus before they started behaving parentally.

A team at the California Primate Research Center at Davis headed by Gary Mitchell and William Redican reviewed their results with adult male–infant pairs of rhesus monkeys in an article that appeared in the April 1974 issue of *Psychology Today*. The team had to be par-

Female rhesus monkey mothering newborn infant. Courtesy of William K. Redican, Gary Mitchell, and Jody Gomber, University of California, Davis.

Male adult rhesus monkeys typically treat infants with indifference if not hostility. The persistence of a helpless baby unlocks patterns of parental behavior. Here, a male rhesus monkey "mothers" (*left*) and grooms (*below*) a month-old infant shortly after the two were left alone together in the cage. Courtesy of William K. Redican, Gary Mitchell, and Jody Gomber, University of California, Davis.

ticularly cautious in setting up the experiments since male rhesus monkeys are often quite hostile toward infant monkeys, sometimes to the point of killing them. The researchers found that when a male adult and a baby lived alone together in a cage, the adult male groomed, played with, and attended to the youngster effectively. To be sure, there were some style differences in the way male and female monkeys practiced parentalism — each of the males romped more often and more roughly with his charge than a monkey mother normally does, and the bond between adult male and youngster seemed to increase over time instead of gradually weakening — but so far the four young monkeys raised by males have turned out to be quite as normal as those raised by females.

The prenatal sex hormone mix apparently does not create any new brain pathways or eliminate any that would otherwise be there. The wiring for all the affected behavior is present in both sexes. What your prenatal mix did was to lower the threshold so that it takes less of a push to switch you on to some behavior and to raise the threshold so that it takes more of a push to switch you on to other kinds. More androgen prenatally means that it takes *less* stimulus to evoke your response as far as strenuous physical activity or challenging your peers is concerned, and *more* stimulus to evoke your response to the helpless young, than would otherwise be the case. *How* you respond once you're over the threshold depends on many things — your age, health, strength, physical development, cultural heritage, gender schemas, environment, training, and experience — but not simply on your prenatal sex hormone exposure.

Prenatally determined differences in sensitivity to

stimuli help to explain why dominance behavior and activities involving a high expenditure of physical energy are more characteristic of boys' play than of girls', and why parental behavior is more characteristic of girls' play than of boys'. When nativists of the "anatomy is destiny" school and sex chauvinists cite this difference as evidence that men are predestined to be active and dominant, women to be passive and nurturant, however, they ignore the fact that all these behaviors are characteristic of both sexes, and they discount the heavy cultural reinforcement that maximizes the original slight difference in the thresholds.

It's not hard to find sources of those cultural reinforcements in the rigid conditions for survival that governed many species, including, for much of its history, the human species. If mother's milk is the only nourishment for an infant, a species can survive only if adult females stay close to the young to breast-feed until the young can manage whatever the adult food may be. And if survival depends on killing dangerous prey and predators, the other adults, the males, must be willing to leave the young to hunt and fight. Early humans had to hunt far and fast, and when they had no weapons but muscle, speed, skill, and teamwork, they had to have their teamwork down to split second precision, with any question about who was directing the team settled beforehand. These conditions no longer govern our survival, but their influence is perpetuated in average differences between men and women collectively in size and muscular strength, in the prenatal sex hormone effect on brain pathways, and in cultural traditions including language, as will be discussed in Chapter 4.

The nativists and sex chauvinists are right to the extent that if cultural influences were neutralized, one would still expect to find more men than women among those

79

striving for dominance and those who prefer activities that demand a high expenditure of physical energy, and more women than men among those who prefer child care to other kinds of work. The prenatal sex hormone mix would still influence preferences. The point is that society need no longer insist that for a man to be a man he must be active and dominant, or for a woman to be a woman she must be passive and nurturant, no matter what capabilities and potential the interaction of nature and nurture may have given them. We can afford to relax gender stereotypes to permit far more freedom in individual development, and in fact we can't afford not to do so. Human survival today depends to a terrifying extent on the cooperation of people as responsible members of the human race, but not at all on hunting, fighting, and breast-feeding.

What these discoveries boil down to is that, very early in your life, your sex differentiation equipped you for, or barred you from, either impregnating on the one hand, or menstruating, gestating, and lactating on the other, later in your life. The painstaking detective work we have outlined points to the conclusion that the prenatal sex hormones triggered the development in you — whether you are male or female — of the potential for strenuous physical activity, dominance behavior, and parental behavior. If you had the higher percentage of androgen in that prenatal mix that males normally have, the potential for strenuous physical activity and dominance behavior was later apt to be more sensitive, would respond to weaker stimuli, than if you had less androgen. And if you did not have that higher percentage of androgen in your prenatal mix, your potential for parental behavior, which all of us have, tended to remain somewhat more sensitive to the stimuli that evoke it than if you had had more androgen prenatally. After you were born, environmental influences increased or decreased your sensitivity to stimuli that elicit behavior of various kinds, so that the sex differences created by the prenatal sex hormone mix were either maximized, equalized, or minimized, depending on your environment. In the United States, the main cultural effect is to reinforce and maximize sexual differences. What the prenatal sex hormone mix did *not* do was to preordain sexual differences in you in an immutable formula that would either equip or bar you from strenuous physical activity, dominance behavior, or parental behavior.

If the prenatal sex hormone mix creates differences in brain pathways other than sensitivity to stimuli to these three kinds of behavior, it would be very useful to know what those other differences are. A great many of the sex differences long assumed to be inborn have turned out to be historically determined options; others still inspire hot debate but no conclusions. For example, that there is a difference between the sexes in native intelligence has been widely accepted as an eternal verity, but never proved, nor is it likely to be proved. Before anyone can determine whether boys and girls differ nativistically in, say, mathematical intelligence, it will be necessary to have a cultural environment in which the sexes are not culturally stereotyped as being different in mathematical ability. This is not to deny the possibility of a nativistic difference. There might be one, and it might one day be shown to be derived from the Adam principle, insofar as a higher percentage of male sex hormone in prenatal development may give boys an advantage in spatial ability, which may be related to the subsequent male role in pegging out territory and defending its boundaries, or in being erotically aroused by visual imagery. But all of this speculation is, at the present time, pure science fiction. It can't be proved.

One is defeated at the outset in trying to demonstrate a sex difference in intelligence if one assumes that intelligence is some sort of pure essence. Like many other traits, intelligence is an abstract and rather amorphous concept that can be deduced only by inference. The psychologist who administers an intelligence test does not, in any real sense, measure intelligence; what's measured is behavior — what people do or say, and their quickness in doing or saying it, when they're asked to solve a problem by either making something or saying something in response.

Measuring intelligence poses the same kinds of problem as measuring language ability. It is absolutely impossible to measure the language ability of a child six months of age. One must wait until the baby has reached the developmental stage of beginning to talk. At that stage, the baby needs the stimulus and the social feedback of talk from and with other people. A child reared in social isolation with two deaf-mute parents does not learn to talk. Even though he may learn his parents' sign language, he does not learn vocal language. There's no way of testing his vocal linguistic ability by testing him in sign language, for the two languages, though similar, are not identical in syntax and inflection, to say nothing of the difference between making sounds and hand signs.

Ability in vocal language cannot be measured separately from competence in the use of vocal language. That is, ability and achievement are both part of the same package. You may think of ability as native ability, and you may think of achievement as a product of cultural or social opportunity, but you cannot test them separately.

There is no test for ability without achievement, and no test for achievement without ability. This is true for written language and reading, as well as for spoken language and listening. In fact, it is true for any aspect of human behavior that you may want to test, including intelligence and spatial abilities.

Imagine a self-supporting community in which one of the most sacred rules is that boys and men must keep the vow of silence, where communication by talking is the duty of girls and women, and allowable to them only. In that community it would be impossible to decide whether the males were innately inferior to the females with respect to speech or whether they were simply undeveloped because of the cultural sanction of silence. The only way to resolve the issue would be to take a generation of babies and equalize the opportunity for the boys and girls to learn to talk. It would be a formidable task in a society in which all the older male models either obeyed the sacred vow of silence, or tried falteringly to break out of it!

Elinor Keenan described almost such a community in a paper read to a conference on the ethnography of speaking held at the University of Texas in 1972, cited by Peter Farb (1974). Among the Vakinankaratra of Madagascar, she reported, the behavioral ideal is to avoid confrontation. As in our society, the male, not the female, stereotype corresponds to the ideal, so that the duty of scolding the children, accusing other members of the community of misbehavior, haggling, and the like, devolves upon the women. A man can buy only fixed-price items, and when a man has a quarrel with another man, his female relatives are the champions who do verbal battle for him. When the carnage is over, he steps graciously forward to soothe hurt feelings. If you grew up among the Vakinankaratra, it would be hard to escape the conviction that women are hard-nosed, aggressive, and quarrelsome by nature, and that tact and amiability are male traits.

The parallel with intelligence and other assumed sex differences is obvious. Our society has a millennial history of sex-stereotyping intelligent behavior. In the history of the Christian church, for example, men are the intelligent builders of logical systems of theology. Women are to perform devotional rituals or have ecstatic visions or revelations (though not to the exclusion of men). In the history of education, it is a very modern idea that girls should be academically educated at all, and a still newer idea that men and women may be so similar in academic intelligence as to be able to compete together. In the current folklore of behavioral science, women are intuitive whereas men are empirical; women are verbal whereas men are mathematical; women are cataloguers whereas men are conceptualizers; women are emotional whereas men are logical; women are perceptive whereas men are creative; and so on.

These sex stereotypes are a random assortment of antitheses that partly contradict one another. They are too abstract and amorphous for concise operational definition, much less scientific testing. But above all, they are stereotypes for which there is today no known way of ascertaining whether a sex difference, provided it can be pinned down, is nativistically or culturally determined.

What can be proved is that many girls and women in competition with boys and men achieve equally well. The opposite also holds true. A society does not, therefore, need to know how many members of one sex can excel at the activities assigned stereotypically to the other sex. It is enough to know that some can excel in order to give them social permission to do so, and thus set an example for younger ones to follow, should it suit them. No one should presume to have authority to force all women, by edict, to do what men more often do, nor all men to do what women more often do. It is enough simply to open the options so that people can perform intellectually in the manner most congenial to them. Then, one day, with options replacing forced stereotypes, it may be possible to find out if there are some native male-female differences in intellect. If some are found, it's highly unlikely that they will be found to be universal. If there are any, they are most probably like sex differences in physique, simply a matter of averages, with many individual exceptions.

4. Gender Identity

THE CHANCES ARE THAT SOCIETY had nothing to do with the turnings you took in the prenatal sex development road, but the minute you were born, society took over. When the drama of your birth reached its climax, you were promptly greeted with the glad ritual cry, "It's a boy!" or "It's a girl!" depending on whether or not those in attendance observed a penis in your crotch. The chances are very high that the salute was appropriate, although, as we have seen, the molding of an infant's external genitals is not quite infallible as an index of prenatal sex differentiation, nor is it invariably accurate as a guide to future turnings. The label "boy" or "girl," however, has tremendous force as a self-fulfilling prophecy, for it throws the full weight of society to one side or the other as the newborn heads for the gender identity fork, and the most decisive sex turning point of all. Parents react differently to the signal "son" or "daughter" from the first moment, and even case-hardened nurses and obstetricians are likely to speak more softly to a newborn baby labeled "girl" and handle her more gently than one who is labeled "boy."

Soon after birth your sex was entered on your birth certificate, one more link in the gender chain. Then your name was picked, most likely a gender-coded one. Your parents spread the glad tidings of your arrival far and wide, using your name and those pervasive pronouns "he" or "she," "him" or "her," and perhaps resorting to a pink or blue color scheme to make sure that even strangers would know whether to react to you as a boy or girl. They started dressing you in boy- or girl-type clothes only a few weeks later, long before different kinds of pants could serve any practical purpose. Their concept of you as a boy or a girl, backed by everybody else in your world, pressed relentlessly upon you.

As your mind and body developed according to the universal developmental stereotype for the human species — modified, of course, by your particular social heritage and family environment — the interaction of all these forces was creating a unique individual. The more strength and control you gained, the more you became one of the forces shaping your own unique destiny, a force that was amplified in reflection back and forth as you influenced those around you and the way they reacted to you. But whatever the status of your chromosomes, hormones, sex organs, and individuality, their directional push was no match for societal pressures when it came to differentiating your gender identity.

There's no bypassing the gender identity fork. It is practically impossible for a person to develop any sense identity at all without identifying as either a male or a female, and the gender identity gate locks firmly behind. Yet in a very special way, this fork must be straddled. You had to construct both male and female internal models — schemas — in your brain, concepts of what it means to be male and what it means to be female. The importance of that other schema, the one that doesn't match your gender identity, and the use you make of it, are only beginning to be appreciated.

Soon after you were born these schemas, or mental constructs, began forming in your brain, based on observation, training, precept, and your own experience of yourself. You got the outlines from your immediate family; first from your mother, then from your father, brothers, and sisters, or from whoever stood in those relationships to you at the time, and from the broader reaches of society as your horizon expanded. One of these schemas tells you what to expect of yourself and how to relate to those of your own sex. The other tells you what to expect of and how to react to those around you of the opposite sex. Together your schemas largely define your identity and gender role.

You attained your gender identity/role in much the same way you attained speech. In fact, the parallel with language illustrates the way gender identity/role develops. You were born wired for language, so to speak, but not programmed for any particular language. You couldn't have learned to talk unless you'd been born with the mouth, vocal chords, ears, and brain pathways to accommodate language, but these were not enough. There also had to be the releasing stimulus of an environmental example, and it had to come at the right time in your life.

Reports of children isolated from other humans or reared among deaf-mutes indicate that those children did not spontaneously learn to talk. The isolated children who were later brought back into the talking community did not learn to use language proficiently.

The environmental trigger that enabled you to start talking was the use of language by those around you during that critical language-learning period, the first few years after your birth. It was interaction between your prenatally programmed disposition for language and the postnatal, socially programmed language signals you heard that made it possible. You couldn't have become a talking person unless somebody talked a language to you. Furthermore, the language that was talked to you then put its mark on the way you could talk and the way you could think ever after. It became your native language and will always be your native language, even if you never used it afterward.

Because gender identity differentiates before a child can talk about it, the assumption has been that it is inborn. But it is not. You were born with something that was ready to become your gender identity. You were wired but not programmed for gender in the same sense that you were wired but not programmed for language. Your gender identity couldn't differentiate as male or female without social stimulation any more than the undifferentiated gonad you started out with could have become testicles or ovaries without the stimulation of your Y or X chromosomes. The interaction between your inborn disposition for gender and the gender signals that came to you in your first few years of postnatal life enabled you to identify yourself as male or female. Furthermore, the gender you identified with then became your native gender

89

and would remain so whatever you might do or whatever fate might decree for you thereafter. It's true that prenatal hormones lowered your threshold for some kinds of behavior, and it's true that the vocal chords you were born with could more easily form some kinds of sounds than others. Your particular vocal chords still lend a flavor to your speech, and your prenatal sex hormone exposure still lends a flavor to your expression of your masculinity or femininity, but your vocal chords didn't determine whether you would speak Chinese or English, and your prenatal sex hormones didn't determine whether you would identify yourself as male or female, nor did anything else that happened to you before you were born.

When you see a transexual like Jan Morris, Christine Jorgensen, or Roberta Cowell, it's no use asking, "Is she *really* still a man, or was she *really* a woman all those years?" The question is meaningless. All you can say is that this is a person whose sex organs differentiated as male and whose gender identity differentiated as female. Medical science has found ways to reduce the incompatibility by modifying anatomy to help that person achieve unity as a member of a sex, just as it has helped the baby described below to achieve unity by modifying the differentiation of gender identity, but medical science has not yet found a way to modify a fully differentiated gender identity.

Convincing evidence that the gender identity gate was wide open when you were born and stayed open for some time thereafter can be found in matched pairs of hermaphrodites. You'll remember that these pairs were formed by matching the files of two people who were sexually concordant at birth, one of them assigned by society as male, the other as female. Only a few years from the same sexual start, one of each pair has become a boy, the other a girl. They develop into men and women as different from each other as normal men are different from normal women.

But is the gate also open for those who were sexually normal at birth? Transexuals give the answer — yes. They are people who, by the criterion of today's tests, were anatomically and hormonally normal males or females at birth and were officially labeled as such. With all the pre-natal sex determinants hanging together to steer them in the direction of their labels, they still went the other way at the gender identity fork. All the available evidence points to the conclusion that this incompatible turn was directed by undercover signals from society, usually rep-resented in early postnatal life by the mother. If there is a genetic or hormonal factor, pre- or postnatal, that predisposes some people toward transexualism, diligent research has not yet found it.

Dramatic proof that the gender identity option is open at birth for normal infants and that social forces can inter-vene decisively at least up to a year and a half after birth comes from a few unusual cases such as one that occurred more than ten years ago.

A young farm couple took their sturdy, normal, identi-cal twin boys to a physician in a nearby hospital to be circumcised when the boys were seven months old. The physician elected to use an electric cauterizing needle instead of a scalpel to remove the foreskin of the twin who chanced to be brought into the operating room first. When this baby's foreskin didn't give on the first try, or on the second, the doctor stepped up the current. On the third try, the surge of heat from the electricity literally cooked the baby's penis. Unable to heal, the penis dried up, and in a few days sloughed off completely, like the stub of an umbilical cord.

When the parents saw what had happened they were stunned, and as soon as the baby could leave the hospital they took him home. They had no idea of where to turn for help, and they were so numbed by the catastrophe that they could hardly talk about it, even with each other. Eventually they recovered themselves enough to make inquiries, but the problem was beyond the experience of their local doctors. Finally they took the baby to a famous medical center, but even there no help was forthcoming. They went back home without hope, their slender finances drained and they themselves almost paralyzed by the frustration of not knowing what to do. The father began having nightmares in which he attacked a doctor and shot him dead.

A plastic surgeon who knew of the Johns Hopkins program for helping hermaphroditic babies finally was called in as a consultant. He suggested the possibility of reassigning the baby as a girl. This was a new and frightening idea to the parents, and at first they shied away from it. Not long afterward, however, they happened to tune in on the last part of a television program about the work with transexuals at Johns Hopkins. On the screen was an adult male-to-female transexual who, they could see for themselves, looked and talked like a normal, attractive woman. After that they worked their way to the decision to reassign their son as a girl. They began using a girl's name, letting the child's hair grow, and choosing noncommittal clothes for this twin. A short time later, when the twins were seventeen months old, they made the trip to Johns Hopkins. They needed reassurance that the program they had undertaken was the right thing for the child, and they wanted the necessary treatment from a hospital that was far enough from home to minimize the risk that gossip would leak back to their community.

The professional resources of the Johns Hopkins Hospital and specialty clinics were promptly mobilized to assess the possible alternatives. The first thing to consider was the child's gender identity. From conception to the age of fifteen months, every force had consistently steered this child toward differentiation of a male gender identity, except that, from the age of seven months, there had been no penis to confirm the other sex determinants. However, since the child had only just begun to talk when the parents had decided on reassignment, there was an excellent chance that gender identity would not by then have differentiated very far in the male direction. That was encouraging, but there was also the question of the parents' expectations. For fifteen months, this child had been their son; could they make the difficult adjustment of accepting the same child as their daughter? It was a vital consideration, for any lingering doubts whatsoever in their minds would weaken the child's identification as a girl and woman.

The medical psychologist described the alternatives to the parents, using nontechnical words, diagrams, and photographs of children who had been reassigned. On the one hand, he explained, if the child grew up as a boy, a plastic surgeon could graft skin from the child's belly to fashion a penis. Female-to-male transexuals had found, however, that after this kind of operation the tissues of the artificial penis often break down, allowing leakage during urination, and that the artificial urethral canal is not very good at resisting the inward advance of infection, which increases the danger of urinary and bladder infec-

93

tions. Another problem is that, since a skin graft penis has no touch or pain feelings, continuous care must be exercised to make sure that it does not become ulcerated by rubbing against clothing, or being bruised or squeezed. The most serious drawback, however, is that it has no sexual feeling and cannot erect. As a man, this child's testicles could generate the sperm to sire his own children, but it would be difficult to ejaculate them into the vagina, since he would have to use an artificial penis support for sexual intercourse and would not experience the normal frictional sensations that produce orgasm.

On the other hand, if the parents stood by their decision to reassign the child as a girl, surgeons could remove the testicles and construct feminine external genitals immediately. When she was eleven or twelve years old, she could be given the female hormones that would normally feminize her body for the rest of her life. Later a vaginal canal could be surgically constructed so that her genitals would be adequate for sexual intercourse and for sexual pleasure, including orgasm. She could become as good a mother as any other woman, but only by adoption.

The medical psychologist stressed that there would be no turning back once gender identity had differentiated. The child was still young enough so that whichever assignment was made, erotic interest would almost certainly direct itself toward the opposite sex later on, but the time for reaching a final decision was already short. He explained that whichever way they decided, it was essential that they decide wholeheartedly; the child would need all their support in differentiating a gender identity, and any lingering doubts in their minds would undermine that support.

Though not highly educated, the twins' parents are

intelligent and exceptionally sensible people. They quickly grasped the risk of delay and of mental reservations, however well concealed, about the child's sex. With the alternatives thus spelled out, they reconfirmed their decision on sex reassignment: The child would be a girl. They had reached the conclusion of an agonizing decision in favor of castration. The girl's subsequent history proves how well all three of them succeeded in adjusting to that decision.

There was also the twin brother to be considered. When a baby is sex-reassigned, it is easy for a sibling to get the notion that a child's sex is one of those things grown-ups switch around at their whim, a notion that would seriously threaten any child's security in his or her own gender identity. In the present instance, the twin brother was too young at the time to remember his sister's reassignment, and the parents have since done well in protecting his conviction that he most certainly is a boy who is growing up to be a man. Both of the children will be given the full story, step by step, as they grow older. Not to give them the complete story would be dangerous in view of the number of documents the children will eventually come to possess. Also, there are many people who know about this case and who might sometime make an unauthorized disclosure to the children, either deliberately or inadvertently.

Even if there has been no publicity, relatives, friends, and neighbors pose a problem whenever a child's sex has to be reassigned. This may seem a trivial matter in comparison with the other problems, and one might assume that the less said the better. Unsatisfied curiosity, however, is a time bomb that ticks on, eroding a family's peace of mind whether or not it ever explodes. One solution is to move to a new community where the baby's history is not known, but the economic cost of making such a move is often prohibitive, and the emotional cost of cutting all ties with family and friends is both extreme and unnecessary. Furthermore, moving away leaves open the possibility that some chance encounter will eventually raise awkward questions concerning any forbidden secret of the past.

For parents who don't feel equal to the ordeal of making explanations, the recommendation is to confide the full story to a close friend, or perhaps to a doctor, nurse, teacher, or clergyman, and thereafter refer all questions to that person. One very wise woman whose grandchild was born hermaphroditic and had to be reassigned chose to meet this problem head on. Arming herself with diagrams illustrating how sex organs develop before birth, she returned to her small coastal village to find that her ladies' club had scheduled a meeting for that very night. She went to the meeting, took the floor, and proceeded to educate the women of the village on birth defects of the sex organs and their treatment. She concluded by explaining that since some infants are sexually unfinished when they're born, the first announcement of a child's sex can be mistaken. "That's what happened with my grandchild," she told them, "and, for the sake of the baby's future, I don't want to hear any more about it." She never did, nor did anyone else in that family. With their curiosity satisfied, the townspeople accepted the event, sympathized as they would with any medical emergency of a neighbor, and made it a point to protect the baby's future by never mentioning it.

In the case of the twins, the parents recognized that moving away from their farm and family in an attempt to obliterate the past was not the answer. Being a forthright person, their mother met the challenge as soon as they got home. Painful as it was, she elected to tell their relatives, friends, and neighbors as much as they wanted or needed to know of the story rather than leaving it to someone else.

At the age of twenty-one months, the little girl was brought back to Johns Hopkins for the first stage of surgical feminization, removal of testicles and feminization of external genitals. When her body reaches adult size, she can decide when to schedule construction of the vaginal canal. If she waits until shortly before she is ready to begin her sex life, sexual intercourse will help to keep the canal elastic and unconstricted. Meanwhile, there's nothing about her genital appearance to make her feel self-conscious, even if she gets into the bathtub with her twin brother.

The twins and their parents come back to Johns Hopkins once a year for general psychological counseling and a checkup. Although the girl had been the dominant twin in infancy, by the time the children were four years old there was no mistaking which twin was the girl and which the boy. At five, the little girl already preferred dresses to pants, enjoyed wearing her hair ribbons, bracelets and frilly blouses, and loved being her daddy's little sweetheart. Throughout childhood, her stubbornness and the abundant physical energy she shares with her twin brother and expends freely have made her a tomboyish girl, but nonetheless a girl. Her dominance behavior has expressed itself in fussing over her brother, according to their parents, "like a mother hen," while he, in turn, takes up for his sister if he thinks anyone is threatening her. Their mother reported that dolls and a doll carriage

97

headed her Christmas list when she was five and that, quite unlike her brother, the girl was neat and dainty, experimented happily with styles for her long hair, and often tried to help in the kitchen.

Although this girl is not yet a woman, her record to date offers convincing evidence that the gender identity gate is open at birth for a normal child no less than for one born with unfinished sex organs or one who was prenatally over- or underexposed to androgen, and that it stays open at least for something over a year after birth.

To show that the gender identity gate locks tight once it closes, there is the evidence of transexuals. When it comes to an all-out tug-of-war between a normal-appearing adult body of one sex and a differentiated gender identity of the other sex in the same person, the gender identity wins hands down. Never yet has even the full weight of societal pressure, abetted by intensive psychotherapy, been able to reverse the gender identity of a transexual after it had differentiated completely.

For evidence that the gender identity gate closes before puberty there are the two hermaphrodites described in Chapter 2. Both were under twelve years old when the gender identities they had differentiated were challenged by their bodies, but their gender identities didn't budge for a minute. Each emphatically rejected the suggestion of sex reassignment. Such challenges were far more formidable in the days before medical science could modify the body to match the gender identity. Before hormone therapy became available, a girl whose body began to masculinize at puberty faced the prospect of becoming a tuba-voiced, flat-chested woman who would have to shave her face daily, but the records show that she remained a woman, experiencing herself as a woman even if her clitoris grew to look like a penis and showed an embarrassing tendency to erect. Boys who discovered at puberty that they would go through life with smooth faces, broad hips, full breasts, and high voices did not mistake themselves for women, although other people might.

The subsequent histories of those who have been coerced into sex reassignment after the gender identity gate had closed counsel strongly against presuming to force it open, but there are still those who insist on doing so. Just recently another doctor who should have known better made this same old mistake; after examining a young teenager, he said abruptly to the parents, "You'd better think of a new name for this child — you have a son, not a daughter."

The arguments in favor of such arbitrary sex reassignment usually rest on the importance of preserving presumed fertility. It's true that however much of a problem uncontrolled fertility may have become for society, the value to an individual of his or her own potential fertility cannot be lightly dismissed. When it comes to preserving a person's fertility by sex reassignment after the gender identity gate has closed, however, the argument loses weight. By that time, the direction of the individual's erotic interest has already been set to accord with gender identity. If arbitrarily reassigned, a person must either dissociate from his or her past so completely as to become a psychological cripple or else continue to respond erotically to members of what was formerly seen as the opposite sex, but which must now be acknowledged as the same sex. Emotional instability is a high price to pay for fertility, and how relevant is fertility to a person who is by social definition an obligative homosexual? How useful is fertility likely to be to someone who is decreed to be a man on the basis of male gonads, but who, having identified as a woman, cannot get an erection for a woman? Or to a woman who experiences herself in her own mind as a male and so falls in love with a woman?

Robert Stoller (1968) puts the argument this way:

What about a child, a heterosexually oriented girl, told at the age of 12 that she is really a boy? If we now follow the demands of the "moral" position, we try to change her into a boy. We then find that she is unable to will away her formerly heterosexual orientation which now, by the surgeon's knife and by fiat, makes her into a homosexual. How moral is such morality? . . . On the other hand, if one removes the undescended testes, creates a vagina, and gives estrogens, one has a little girl who can function normally in harmony with what she feels herself to be psychologically, she can have a sexually gratifying life, and if she adopts a child she can mother it appropriately. To maintain that this is morally wrong seems to put one in a position that is not as easy to defend as it may have been 400 years ago.

The importance of gender identity, and the hazards of trying to change it once it has differentiated, make it vitally important to pinpoint the critical period for this stage of development. "Somewhere between fifteen months and the onset of puberty" covers too much time. It hasn't been easy to narrow the bracket. Like other stages of development, this one varies somewhat with the individual. In addition, cultural patterns of child training sometimes obscure the gender differentiation process. We can now say, however, that the critical period for gender identity differentiation coincides with the critical period for learning language, which is much easier to observe.

Two very exceptional Johns Hopkins cases probably mark the extreme upper age limit for the gender identity gate to remain open. While at first glance these two case histories seem to indicate that language can be mastered before gender identity differentiates, in fact they confirm the close connection between the two learning processes.

Each of these two people is a genetic female who was masculinized both before and after birth by adrenal cortex secretions. Each looked more male than female at birth and was labeled male. One of the babies, however, developed severe dehydration and salt loss at the age of two weeks and had to be hospitalized for emergency treatment. Alerted to the possibility of adrenal-cortex malfunction by the baby's condition, the attending doctors discovered the female status of the child's chromosomes, gonads, and internal genitals and advised sex reannouncement. (If the baby's sex label is changed soon after birth, "reannouncement" is the right term. Later, when the child has begun to identify with the first label so that changing it requires the child as well as the family and others to readjust to the new label, the term is "reassignment.") When this baby was recognized as a girl, cortisone treatment was prescribed to counteract the masculinizing influence of her adrenal cortices. Unaccountably, no genital surgical repair was done to make her look like a girl, and nobody suggested that the birth certificate be changed to register her as a girl. The parents, who had little education and no background to help them understand the problem, didn't know what to make of all this. Doubts about the baby's sex lingered in their minds when they took her home to their poverty-stricken farm. Continuing the cortisone treatment soon proved too much for them to cope with, so the child lost even that support for the bodily development of her femininity. She grew to look like a boy.

As for the other child, the male label had gone home with him, along with a warning from the doctor that it might have to be changed later. The parents were given no counseling on how to handle the situation, and they, too, remained doubtful. Uncertainty of this kind is as contagious as measles, and both children contracted it.

The girl was eleven years old when she was first brought to Johns Hopkins. The boy was twelve years old when he came for treatment several years later. Both children were affected by elective mutism on the subject of sex. So painful had the thought of their mixed-up sex become to them that neither child was able to say a word about even such peripherally related topics as clothes. Communication was made still more difficult by the fact that their psychological burdens had interfered with their ability to learn. They could barely read and write.

During interviews, each child would sit quietly, apparently without resentment, while staff members talked about the child's sex problem with the parent, when a parent was there, or with each other. At the mere mention of anything connected with their sex, each of these children became so still as to seem lost in a state of almost catatonic trance.

Under the most favorable circumstances, it usually takes great skill and patience to get a child to discuss sexual problems. Soon after the children of our culture begin to talk, they usually discover that any talk of sex tends to detonate explosions in the ears of any listening adults. They know nothing of privileged communication between doctor and patient. It's hard to convince them that one has nonexplosive ears, and that there will be no penalties or reprisals if they reveal in the consulting room what they have painfully learned to keep to themselves at home. With these two children, it was impossible. Yet before they could be helped, it was imperative to find out how the children really felt about themselves. The person mainly responsible for finding out was the child psychologist.

With each child, the psychologist explained exactly what had happened in the sexual development of his or her body. He used diagrams and words of the crude vernacular familiar to each of them to demystify the explanations. He told them stories and showed them pictures of children with similar problems, both to let them know they were not the only ones who had had to face these difficulties and to get across the message that help was available.

The first session with the boy was quite baffling. According to his mother, he had always tended to keep to himself. He had always dressed as a boy and he usually acted like a boy, but at times his walk and manner would become obviously feminine. He was pleasant and friendly during the session, but the instant the doctor steered the interview toward the direction of sex, the child dropped his head and went blank. He gave no clue that he understood what was said; possibly he simply tuned out so that the words could not reach him. Five weekly sessions later the staff was as baffled as ever. Then, on the morning after the fifth session, a scrap of paper, folded over and over into a grubby little wad, was found lying under the chair he'd been sitting on. On it, this practically illiterate child had written a message as clear and concise as Julius Caesar's "*Veni, vidi, vici.*"

"Dear Doctor, I do not wemt to be a boy. I wemt to be a girl just [like] my sisters."

Reassignment as a girl, with cortisone therapy to counteract the faulty adrenal secretions, allowed this child to start blossoming out. In the spring of the year, she donned girls' clothes and let her hair grow. The hormones from her ovaries, no longer suppressed by the adrenal secretions, caused her breasts to start developing, and that summer she had surgery to reduce the size of her clitoris and exteriorize the internal opening of her vagina. Arrangements had been made for her to stay with an aunt and go to school in another city in order to ease the adjustment, but her morale was so high that she herself elected not to go away. In the fall she went right back to the same special tutorial class at the same school she had attended as a boy.

As her confidence in herself as a girl mounted, her mutism diminished. Eventually she found her tongue to such good effect that she was able to hail a young tough into court for trying to force her to prove her femininity in sexual intercourse. Later she married. She could expect to have children, and looked forward to it, although she did not, as it happened, have the luck to get the pregnancy she wanted, although there was no medical reason for the failure. Some years later when she still had not achieved a pregnancy, she turned for a while to a lesbian affair.

The other member of this matched pair found it even harder to communicate at first. After a few sessions, though, she managed to signal, by nodding and shaking her head, that no, she didn't want to grow up to be a woman and a mommy, and yes, she did want to grow up to be a man. It was clear that she had understood the questions, and that her nods represented her true preference, but her parents, too, had to be convinced. In this case, the parents, having learned from the initial reannouncement that doctors can make mistakes about a child's sex, would not find it easy to consent to sex reassignment unless they were absolutely certain that the child herself wanted it. It was not at all sure that this child would find the courage to confront her parents with her need to be a boy. With unequivocal certainty of the need to do so, the psychologist arranged to interview the child in the presence first of her father, then of her mother.

They were tensely dramatic sessions. In the first one, the father listened while the doctor talked to the child. The child sat silent, doodling and scribbling on a piece of paper for what seemed a very long time. Then, very deliberately, she took a fresh piece of paper and slowly, with intense concentration, traced out for her father this masterpiece of three-letter word communication: "I got to B a Boy."

Once the message was committed to writing, she addressed it formally to "Father," and the father signed it. In a separate session immediately after that, a similar document was achieved and signed by the mother. One serious obstacle had been cleared, but there was still another before reassignment surgery could be scheduled, and that was the question of professional ethics in a case unprecedented as this one was in the experience of most of the personnel involved.

Those who felt misgivings about "altering the sex" of this child by removing the ovaries had to reexamine their definitions of sex. The child who came to the clinic had, on the one hand, female chromosomes and gonads, and a feminine name and label; on the other hand, there was the birth certificate of a male, masculine external genitals, a masculinizing hormone mix, and a male physique. Furthermore, the child's female label had been so ambiguous from birth that it was hard to tell which way the gender identity leaned. For this youngster to become a comfortable member of either sex, some things would have to be altered. Since it is possible to alter anatomy and hormone ratio but not gender identity, finding out which way the child's gender identity inclined was the crucial concern. Which ever way it was leaning, there was almost no chance of reversing the direction, no matter what efforts might be made to change it; and for differentiation to continue in the direction it was tending this child needed all the support that could be provided.

Once agreement on the ethical question and on the gender identity trend had been reached, the reassignment program began. The adrenal secretions that had heavily masculinized the child's body were suppressed by cortisone therapy, since monthly injections of androgen would effectively maintain body masculinity, health and well-being. Surgery was scheduled to remove the ovaries and uterus and to fuse the underside of the unfinished clitorine penis so that the child could urinate in the standing position. Plastic testicles were ordered. These would be inserted for cosmetic effect in the scrotum already formed by the labia, which had fused before the child was born.

Once again the results were heartwarming. The mutism that had been such a handicap to the child as a girl disappeared quite rapidly. He was able to talk before a medical audience, a feat that would have been previously impossible for him as a girl. His schoolwork improved. When he was fifteen years old, he began dating a girl.

Although he is exceptionally short in stature, there's nothing about him now to raise any doubt that he is a young man, and he is certainly a much happier person than the miserable girl who first came to the clinic.

The most extraordinary feature of these two case histories is that, from sexually concordant beginnings at birth and opposite sex assignments, each had begun to differentiate a gender identity contrary to the sex assignment, and each negotiated sex reassignment in late childhood successfully. What made it possible for these two to request and adapt to reassignment was the doubt that had kept their gender identities ambiguous throughout the critical period for gender identity differentiation and after, plus the fact that the new sex assignments corresponded in each case with the direction in which gender identity had predominantly differentiated.

What made their gender identities lean away from, instead of toward, their assigned sex is another question. The ambiguity of their uncorrected genital appearance and the uncertainty in the minds of their parents helped to keep the gate open so that for these children there were three possibilities: male, female, neither. The third possibility is almost unheard of. There are people known to have established a sense of identity without identifying themselves as either male or female, but as partly both, though they are very rare indeed. For anybody, though, if things are bad enough the way they are, almost any change looks like a change for the better. Any girl who is miserable may wish she were a boy and if, like this child, she's not quite sure she really is a girl because of funny-looking genitals and overheard remarks, it would perhaps

107

be easy for her to slip over the line and decide she really *is* a boy, and of course the same line of reasoning applies to boys.

If these two people seem to contradict the proposition that gender identity cannot successfully be reversed after a child achieves a serviceable command of language, they actually offer confirmation. They could talk, but their reading and writing disabilities had so handicapped them that they were, for all intents and purposes, illiterate; and not only could neither of them utter a word about sex, but they were promptly struck dumb at the mention of anything remotely related to sex. The fact that their elective mutism disappeared and their reading and writing difficulties abated after their gender identity problems began to be resolved substantiates the close connection between language and gender identity.

Another case history, that of a boy with a micropenis and an ambivalent but predominantly masculine gender identity, illustrates the connection in a different way. He had not been doing nearly as well as he could have in school until, during his third year of high school, he suddenly began to pick up. "One of the signs of his picking up," the medical psychologist noted in reporting the case,

was that, with unusual rapidity, he began to learn French, and then started writing French verse. At the same time, he wrote English short stories, also. It dawned on me one day that the French verse was very lyrical and feminine, and the English short stories were rough and rugged, with a lot of masculine, assertive imagery in them. In a subsequent interview, I told the boy of my impression, and of my hypothesis that he was laying the foundation for a possibility that if he ever changed to be a girl, he would go to France to live and speak French, while if he made the grade living as a boy, he could continue living in America, speaking English. He said that I was right, and admitted that he had, in fact, already made plans for a year of study-leave in a French institution. This is a rather neat example of how sex and achievement, or underachievement and dropoutism, may tie together. I suspect that there is a lot more we could learn about the relation between sex and dropping out if we became more sensitive to what to look for. This case offered a rare opportunity in that there was a kind of transparency or window through which to observe gender identity differentiation taking place. As far back as the boy can remember, he and his mother were deadlocked in a feud. Not knowing too much about the family factors, I am diffident about my interpretation, but it is this: The mother says, in effect, "Well, if you've got only a little penis, you'd better have a big brain." The boy, having no other active form of ammunition with which to fight his mother when he needed to assert himself, used the ready-made ammunition of omitting to use his brain for academic achievement.

It is not mere coincidence that the critical period for gender identity differentiation coincides with the critical period for acquiring language. The connection can be found in the origin of conceptual language.

The more complex an organism is, the more its survival depends on communication between its various parts. Among various animal species including the human race, grunts, whistles, squeaks, groans, movements, and gestures have long since been employed as signals to facilitate cooperation. As the human species evolved its greater brain capacity, it became possible for human beings to develop these cries for help, warnings of danger, tidings of food and water, threats, and mating signals into increasingly elaborate systems of communications. In the widely accepted view, conceptual language evolved out of such oral animal signals.

Yet it is equally plausible to assume that conceptual language, language as we know it today, did not evolve at all, but rather that during a brief critical period at the beginning of civilization it was quite deliberately invented, as modern mathematical language has been invented. And it is a plausible conclusion that conceptual language as we know it was invented, not for the purpose of communication, but to help some human beings gain and hold power over other human beings. Startling as these propositions may be, there is much to support them.

There is reason to believe that the human brain had attained its present capacity as far back as Cromagnon times, twenty-five thousand or more years ago. The marvelous cave drawings discovered near Altamira in Spain and Lascaux in France are known to be more than eleven thousand years old. If we could measure the IQ of the cave painters and their forebears, we would doubtless find their scores the equal of ours. And what were our brainy ancestors doing with all that intellectual capacity? Inventing. They were devising speedier and more dependable ways to meet the stiff environmental challenges to their survival than the method of natural physical selection. The outsize human brain was replacing all the rest of the body as the human instrument of adaptation to the hostile environment. Prehistoric human beings tamed fire and brought it inside the cave to protect themselves from the deadly environmental cold, made weapons for hunting and tools for cultivating to secure a food supply when the environment grew stingy. They invented axes to create shelter where the environment provided none, pots to keep food in, knives to shape things — and symbols to communicate with.

Other species may have shared with early humans the

ability to signal to their fellows something of what was happening at the moment, but human beings, alone in the animal kingdom, invented ways to communicate a memory of what had happened yesterday, or on the other side of the mountain — ways to pool information gathered at different times and places.

A body of information confers the power to generalize, to trace the thread that weaves certain forces, objects, and events into a pattern of cause and effect. The body of information that can be assembled without the aid of records is meager and questionable, but it was enough to give preliterate humanity a taste for generalization, and generalization is headier than alcohol. Recognition of a cause-effect pattern enables one to predict the probable effect whenever particular forces converge, to discern a repetitive sequence which we now call natural law. Those who grasp it can at least prepare for and sometimes control the outcome. They can, in some particular situations, predict. The long, slow process of replacing magic with science could begin.

The first generalizers must have gained enormous power. However shaky their data base, however far they might stretch a modest generalization, however slight the control they thus gained over destiny, it was more than anyone had ever had before. One can only guess at how those early generalizers used their power, but sighting back along six thousand years of recorded history points to the conclusion that they used it to increase and extend their power. And how better protect the source of that power, the accumulated knowledge of cause and effect, than by building walls of secrecy so that only those chosen for initiation into the secret can tap the power? Such walls can be fashioned of words.

Hints that language has been associated with power from the beginning can be found in the roots of many languages. The old Anglo-Saxon phrase for "to speak," for example, was "to unlock the word hoard" (Laird, 1953). The ancient Norsemen attributed magical powers to their Runic letters. It is written in the Bible, "In the beginning was the Word, and the Word was with God, and the Word was God."

"In 1492," wrote Peter Farb in *Word Play* (1974),

Queen Isabella of Spain was formally presented with a copy of Antonio de Nebrija's *Gramatica*, the first grammar written about any modern European language. When the queen bluntly asked, "What is the book for?" the Bishop of Avila replied: "Your Majesty, language is the perfect instrument of Empire." Language and the state, as the bishop wisely said, have been companions throughout history.

As for the hypothesis that language was used to create and maintain an elite, the evidence is even stronger. People are constantly inventing languages, ingenious codes shared by "us" to exclude "them." Each new generation of youngsters gleefully experiments with some form of pig Latin, op- or bop-language. Gangsters, hippies, addicts, and practically every other subgroup quickly evolve their own jargons. For others there are, as there have been throughout history, the innumerable clubs, fraternities, orders, knights of this, and daughters of that, each with its cabalistic passwords and incantations. The professions still use language to protect power, and every doctor, lawyer, priest, scientist, and mathematician has to learn, along with the specialized vocabulary needed for precision, a welter of semantic formulas for the sole purpose of maintaining the aura of mystery that shuts out the layman.

When John Weightman reviewed Stanislav Andreski's book *Social Science as Sorcery* for the *Washington Post* (July 13, 1973), he made this pertinent comment:

What passes for sociological thought in the works of many contemporary exponents is a mystificatory use of jargon, sometimes innocent, sometimes more sinister. . . . What Andreski sees as the peculiar vice of sociology, I look upon as the permanent temptations. . . . The human appetite for myth, false certainties and mumbo-jumbo is perpetually reborn in different forms, indeed, one constantly discovers it in oneself.

An editorial in that same issue of the *Post* complained about "the ancient bureaucratic walls of secrecy, intricacy, obscurity and technicality" that surround government regulations, insurance policies, and tax manuals.

Most linguistic authorities assume that languages evolved gradually from simple signals to a peak or plateau of complexity, held there perhaps for a long period, and as gradually devolved in a curve something like this:

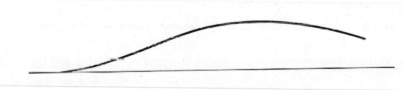

Writing must have come in at some point on the downward slope six thousand or more years ago. If language did indeed evolve this way, then that evolutionary process covered its tracks remarkably well. Anthropologists have ransacked the darkest pockets of civilization around the world in search of a primitive language, but have never yet found one. Even tribes that apparently live the same way their Stone Age ancestors lived have elaborate, intricate languages. The plain fact is that the further back one goes, the more complicated a language becomes, as any student wrestling with classical Latin, Greek, or Sanskrit can attest. Sumerian records of six thousand years ago, the most ancient writings yet unearthed, leave little doubt that language has steadily devolved, and is still devolving.

But if language was invented, the developmental curve would show up more like this:

the same kind of curve that describes the invention of writing.

Our scenario reads thus. Survival required pooling for the tribe's benefit the little store of information each human member could acquire during a short lifetime. The rudiments of language provided a container that held the information together. Then, as information accumulated, a few of the more nimble-witted began to discern recurrent cause-effect patterns, to generalize from them, and to use the generalizations as a basis for assessing the future. Their predictions didn't have to be accurate; as long as they were even a little more accurate than random guesses, or than predictions based on a single individual's own personal experience, the generalizations conferred great power. The early generalizers were held — and quickly learned to hold themselves — in awe, becoming the witch doctors, the priest-rulers, of the tribe, and set about augmenting their power.

An effective way to augment their power was to inflate their generalities extravagantly, a tendency that persists today. Since any generality readily takes on the character of an eternal verity, it's quite easy to magnify a small, limited cause-effect pattern taken from a specific set of circumstances into a grandiose all-encompassing "law of nature," or "law of God." By the time writing was invented, generality inflation had become a fine art. On a tiny base of observed fact, the wily old priest-rulers had managed to construct incredibly elaborate systems of law and theology that gave them control over every detail of their subjects' lives. And when nature or God neglected to enforce these "laws," the rulers used their power ruthlessly to do their own enforcing, and invented taboo, guilt, shame, and the doctrine of original sin to keep their people in line.

While extending their power by inflating generalizations, the rulers buried the power source, like the gold at Fort Knox, in thick-walled structures — in language bristling with intricate noun declensions and cases, interwoven verb conjugations, moods, voices, tenses and persons, endings, compounds, phrases, clauses, and rules of grammar. And gender. Recognizing sex linked differences in some plants, most animals, and all humans, they prodigally inflated the concept, assigning gender to everything in sight and to their gods and bogeymen as well. Gender was fashioned into a language tool to consolidate the rulers' power over other men and all women.

And so this far-ranging discourse leads back, from a different direction, to the gender fork in individual development today, for a generality once accepted as an eternal verity takes on a life of its own. It can survive on the slimmest data base or long after its data base has been swept away by the tides of change. The gender generality legacy, embalmed in language and custom, still weighs heavy on the human race, and since human thought is limited and shaped by language, that legacy still distorts and limits human thinking.

Gender schemas need a firm base in language. This all languages provide, but the trouble is they don't stop there. What's the sense of assigning gender to a table, for example? Obviously none, for tables were feminine to the ancient Greeks and Romans, but masculine to the Teutons. Today the ocean is masculine to Germans but feminine to the French, and so on. Beyond cluttering up languages and making international communication harder than it need be, such arbitrary gender distinctions in themselves perhaps do little harm, but their cumulative effect is to polarize the sexes, to so overstress sex differences that the human similarities are overlooked.

Other gender distinctions in language raise walls between the sexes. In a number of languages, including Japanese, you use a different dialect when speaking to a man than when speaking to a woman. To see how this practically guarantees sex segregation, think of trying to organize a mixed team for work or play, or giving a party, or writing a campaign speech or classroom lecture for a mixed audience under those circumstances. Other gender barriers in language are more subtle. Languages that have only masculine words for professionals and people in positions of importance powerfully reinforce the idea that a woman must reject femininity in order to achieve excellence outside the domestic sphere. In French, a chair, for example, is feminine until it becomes the seat of authority, when it turns masculine. Also, it must give the gender schemas of a French child an odd twist to hear a woman referred to as *le professeur* or a man as *la personne*.

While English is less genderized than the other principal modern languages, it, too, sex-codes concepts that belong in the human schema. Everybody is still "mankind," and anybody is still "he." "The woman on the street" does not mean the average woman, much less the average person. And although most English nouns do not have gender endings, gender seeps back into them through lack of a non-gender-specific third-person-singular pronoun. "It" does very well for animals and sometimes gets by for small children — "Each child got the toy it wanted." Some people resort to using "they" as singular — "Each person chose what they wanted" — but that breach of grammar won't stretch very far; you really couldn't speak of a doctor with "their" patient. Campaigns to degenderize words, like the one to substitute "chairperson" for "chairman," may raise consciousness, but they won't accomplish their stated aim as long as you have to refer back to the person in the chair as "he" or "she," "him" or "her," in the next clause of your sentence. The Turks use "o" as a non-gender-specific third-person pronoun, and we propose it for immediate adoption into English. Among other benefits, such a pronoun would do away with the need for all the tedious "he or she" phrases that slow up a book like this one.

We can afford to go much further with degenderizing English. As firm a foundation for gender schemas is laid in the English language as in the sex organs themselves. A baby born to English-speaking parents has ample opportunity to learn that he or she is a boy or a girl with a father and a mother, and that another immediate relative is either a brother or a sister, uncle or aunt, grandpa or grandma. Later the child can learn that there are roosters and hens, bulls and cows, and so on. There's no danger that broadening the foundation for the human schema will unsex us, but it is frightening that concepts essential to human survival find expression in phrases like "the brotherhood of man," which tell half the people in the world that it's no concern of theirs.

5. Childhood

WHEN THE GENDER IDENTITY GATE CLOSED behind you it locked tight. You knew in the very core of your consciousness that you were male or female. Nothing short of disaster could ever again shake that conviction, and this happened before you got three, or at most four, candles on your birthday cake. As we have seen, the gender identity option may stay open a little longer than that for some hermaphrodites and possibly for a few of those who eventually become transexuals or obligative homosexuals, but only a transvestite with two personalities and two gender identities can reverse direction after the first few years.

Meanwhile, however, you had been gathering impressions of the people around you, impressions that formed your outline of what it means to be a person. Gradually, hazily, you began sorting some of these impressions according to the differences you perceived between the males and the females in your environment. Your first two models were of course your mother and father, or whoever stood in that relationship to you then. They provided the outlines of your two gender schemas, the beginning of your concepts of what is a man and what is a woman. These outlines you expanded and filled in as you went along, the number and variety of models increasing as your horizon expanded. Your emerging sense of identity was your experience of yourself as an individual, a member of the human race, your gender identity was your experience of yourself as male or female.

When your gender identity clicked shut, it left your human schema free but coded one of your gender schemas positive, the other negative. The patterns of behavior that you perceived and fitted into one or the other gender schema acquired whichever coding your gender identity had put on that schema, so that whenever you achieved the ability to put into practice a sex-coded pattern of behavior, you had a guide to whether or not that particular behavior was appropriate for you. If you were a boy you acted like a boy and did boy things because the positive sign gave you the go-ahead for the behavior in your male gender schema. You were boyish also because the negative sign deterred you from doing girl things, the behavior that was in your female gender schema; if you were a girl you got just the opposite steers.

The signs on your schemas were fixed when your gender identity differentiated, your models showed you which behavior to put into which schema. Approval from others told you your sorting of that behavior was correct and reinforced the coding; disapproval told you that you had that behavior in the wrong schema. Conflicting signals from your models confused the issue. Whether or not a particular behavior pattern, once firmly coded, can be transferred to the other schema and recoded, or decoded to go in the human schema, depends on how deeply it has become embedded in your gender identity/role.

The comparatively smooth, straight stretch of development between your early childhood and puberty has been called the latent period on the theory that not much goes on in the way of gender differentiation during those years, but they are not as sexually neutral as the adjective "latent" implies. It's true that sex hormone output, which plays such a dramatic part in prenatal sexual differentiation and again at puberty, doesn't differ significantly in boys and girls from shortly after birth until the onset of puberty. And it's true that while, up to the age of five, boys are on the average a little bigger than girls, between five and ten the differences between the sexes in height, weight, and body build are negligible. Girls enter puberty a year or two earlier than boys, and at about age eleven start shooting up ahead of the boys in height; but during the so-called latent period, the significant sex differentiation that takes place is in the sorting of behavior into male or female schema, a process that manifests itself in play.

Nature-nurture speculation about whether or what kind of sex differences in play behavior would emerge in the absence of parental direction is futile since a child can't survive without at the very least one parent figure to interact with. Child-parent interaction is as inevitable in the differentiation of behavioral differences between the sexes as is interaction between hormones and gonads in the differentiation of gonads into ovaries or testicles.

It's hard to appreciate how many patterns of behavior get sex-coded unless you've tried sex impersonation seriously. As a child, you probably liked to dress up as the opposite sex, and you may still enjoy cross-dressing for a masquerade party or carnival, but the chances are you couldn't have fooled anybody since you were four or five years old. You might perhaps manage to look the part, but you'd find that any number of trifling, apparently quite insignificant gestures, mannerisms, and postures, which never register at all unless they're out of the usual context, would give you away. In *Huckleberry Finn,* Mark Twain has Huck don a long dress and a sunbonnet and behave very quietly in a desperate attempt to pass himself off as a girl, but an old lady easily penetrates his disguise simply by tossing a small object into his lap. When Huck catches it by clamping his knees together instead of spreading his skirt, she knows instantly that he isn't used to wearing skirts.

An expert actor can play opposite-sex roles. In traditional Japanese theater today men still play all the parts, but to make the performance convincing takes a lot of practice over a long period of time. Before women were allowed on the European stage, many male actors specialized in female roles and performed them well. Plots hinging on the successful impersonation of the opposite sex had more credibility in those days than they do now. Shakespeare and other playwrights used them freely. But outside the theater it was never easy, not even in times when the sexes differed far more in dress and behavior than they do today. In addition to learning and practicing the role, you'd need plenty of experience with feedback from others who accept you in that role before you could carry it off without the aid of footlights and a well-drilled cast for support. James Morris discovered this when he became Jan Morris. "We are told that the social gap between the sexes is narrowing," she wrote in her autobiography (1974),

but I can only report that having, in the second half of the twentieth century, experienced life in both roles, there seems to me no aspect of existence, no moment of the day, no contact, no arrangement, no response, which is not different for men and for women. The very tone of voice in which I was now addressed, the very posture of the person next in the queue, the very feel in the air when I entered a room or sat at a restaurant table, constantly emphasized my change of status.

And if others' responses shifted, so did my own. The more I was treated like a woman, the more woman I became. I adapted willy-nilly. If I was assumed to be incompetent at reversing cars or opening bottles, oddly incompetent I found myself becoming. If a case was thought too heavy for me, inexplicably I found it so myself.

While each child, of course, develops at his or her own pace and no group is exactly like another, studies of various groups of children yield the following general picture of the behavior-sorting process during childhood in our culture.

There's not much difference up to the age of thirteen months in the kinds of toys boys and girls choose when offered an assortment. Boys may show partiality for toys that require a lot of banging, but even this difference is slight. Up to age two, children playing in each other's presence don't really play together, but when they do begin to reciprocate in play they don't seem to care whether their playmate is a girl or a boy. By age three, they begin to be aware that boys play with trucks and guns, girls with dolls. When little boys play with dolls, they're more likely to throw the dolls into a cart and trundle around with it than to build a nest for the dolls as girls usually do.

Boys begin to manifest constraint in their play sooner than girls. Little boys are firmer about choosing boy-type playthings when they know they are being watched than when they believe they are alone. When a series of somewhat older boys were each separately asked to construct a setting for a play from a variety of dolls and toy furniture, the doll that figured most often in their constructions was one dressed like a policeman.

Three-year-olds can tell you whether they are girls or boys, but in their play they don't care whether it's a boy or a girl who takes the part of papa, mama, doctor, or nurse. At four, they more uniformly cast themselves in the roles considered appropriate to their sex, and by five they know whether a papa doll or a mama doll represents their own future role.

Somewhere between the age of two and four or five there's an outrageously flirtatious, seductive period when girls play up to their fathers and boys become little swains to their mothers. During this period children often play-act love affairs with each other, making detailed plans for wedding, honeymoon, and home on the range. Later they go through binges of exaggerated modesty. The play love affairs that blossom in kindergarten fade in due course, but love affairs between children eight or more years old have been known to last into adolescence and even into maturity.

If children six or seven years old are asked to draw "a

person," most of them will draw a figure representing their own sex, but the percentage of boys who draw a male figure is higher than the percentage of girls who draw a female figure.

Typical boys' games demand more vigorous expenditure of physical energy and more teamwork than typical girls' games. Boys' games also more often involve throwing and intercepting a ball, which may both reflect and contribute to the fact that males ultimately outnumber females among those above average in ability to solve spatial, mathematical, and mechanical problems.

After kindergarten age, both boys and girls tend to prefer playmates of their own sex, although they will collaborate with members of the other sex for tentative sexual exploration and play if they are not prevented from doing so. The marked preference for playmates of the same sex that characterizes this later childhood period has been interpreted, especially by the children themselves, as a rejection of the opposite sex. Rejection or not, it is a drawing apart in order to concentrate on the schema that matches gender identity and to get practice in expression of the appropriate gender role. Children need to test out their same-sex gender schemas and their performance as boys or girls before undertaking reciprocity with the other sex in adolescence. A boy has an outline of his female schema from his mother and other females in the family. A girl has the outline of a male schema from her father and the other males in the family. Filling in the details of the other-sex schema takes second place during this period while they consolidate their own.

The seduction period of practicing how to complement the parent or parent-figure of the other sex and identify with the parent or parent-figure of the same sex is known in Freudian doctrine as the Oedipal phase. The weakness of most sociopsychological and psychoanalytic studies is that they focus on identification, often leaving complementation out of account altogether. This weakness is serious because the schemas that define gender identity/role are created by the continual interaction between identification and complementation.

If the two people who are a child's first models of maleness and femaleness give mutually contradictory gender signals, the child is handicapped in differentiating concepts of what it is to be male or female. A little boy in roughhouse play not only looks to the father who is his identification model to find out if his behavior is appropriate, but also to the mother who is his complementation model. Approving smiles from both mean that he can fit that behavior firmly into his male schema: Boys roughhouse. Punitive frowns from both leave him on equally firm ground; and not roughhousing goes into his male schema. While this may limit his play, at least he can feel acceptable to both parents when not roughhousing. When he gets around to it, he will note both parents' reactions to a little girl's roughhousing to learn whether or not the behavior belongs in his female schema. If both parents approve roughhousing for girls also, such behavior need not be sex-coded but can go into his human schema: Children roughhouse. But if one parent smiles warmly while the other frowns in anger, it will be very hard for him to feel comfortably male if he roughhouses or if he doesn't, or to react with assurance to girls who do the same.

The sorting process, of course, is the same for girls as for boys. For them the counterpart of roughhousing might be the rehearsal of maternalism — or, more precisely, parentalism. Except for breast-feeding, parental behavior is the same in men and women. The sex difference is in how quickly and easily the behavior can be elicited, but not in its content (see p. 75). It is only good logic, therefore, for both parents to let their children know that both boys and girls can play at rehearsals of parenthood without betraying the proper gender identity and role of either.

Consistency in the signals a child gets from the two parents as to what behavior is acceptable for each sex is essential to his or her development. Schemas can be modified to some extent throughout life, but the early years are the critical period for developing pride and confidence in one's masculinity or femininity. It doesn't matter nearly as much whether the child learns that any particular activity is or is not appropriate behavior for either boys or girls — or both, or neither — as it matters that the two parents mutually agree on the gender acceptability of enough behavior so that the child can feel confident in his performance as a boy or her performance as a girl. Conflicting signals may cause the child to intensify the activity in an effort to get it placed or to shun it altogether, but neither course helps the child.

Encouraging a child to sex-code *all* behavior, however, starves the human schema, so that he or she becomes one of those people who are so overconscious of sex differences that they never notice the human similarities between men and women. The overgenderization of language makes it hard to escape this error. How can a child fail to put laundering into his or her female schema when the only common words for one who launders are washerwoman and laundress? Or keep numerous other activities that belong in the human schema uncoded if there's no third-person-singular pronoun with which to refer to a person who does them, even though the nouns may be sex-neutral? And since language decrees that when sex is not specific, you use the male form — "man" or "mankind" for humanity, "he" for any person unless you particularly mean a female, and so on — the schemas inevitably get lopsided. A recent study of 2,760 stories for young children in 134 schoolbooks from 14 different publishers shows how lopsided. There were men in 147 different occupations in these stories, but women in only 26. Even that is more nearly balanced than the Bible, which, at least in one version, names 3,017 men but only 181 women.

The firmest possible foundations for gender schemas are the differences between male and female genitals and reproductive behavior, a foundation our culture strives mightily to withhold from children. All young primates explore their own and each others' genitals, masturbate, and play at thrusting movements and copulation — and that includes human children, everywhere, as well as subhuman primates. The only thing wrong about these activities is not to enjoy them. But what happens in our culture? Children's sex explorations are treated like a contagious disease. Heroic measures are condoned as soon as the symptoms appear lest the children involved suffer serious damage themselves and spread the contagion to others. Smile at the little boy when he plays at stalking and attacking and the little girl attending to her family of dolls, although the soaring crime rates and population overexpansion menace their future. But don't let them see the incontrovertible differences in their genitals, and don't, at all costs, let them rehearse copulation — the one universal human activity that still imperatively demands that the two sexes behave differently and harmoniously!

Until less than a century ago, children could get at least some idea of genital and copulatory sex differences in behavior from the work and food animals and the pets that were part of their everyday lives. Most of these opportunities were lost when the industrial revolution substituted mechanical horsepower for horses and urbanization separated most families from all other animals except pets. To make matters worse, about the time children started growing up with, at best, perhaps an unmated or spayed dog or cat to demonstrate the "facts of life," their own genital sex differences were being hidden and distorted by many-layered cocoons of clothing.

"Living in the modern world, clothed and muffled," Margaret Mead (1949) gently pointed out,

it is easy to lose sight of the immediacy of the human body plan. The little boy needs to see the changes in body form and hair, the gradually developing genitals, the spreading hair on chest and armpits, the first soft facial down that no razor will recognize, to bind his sense of himself, still so small and undeveloped, to the man that he will become. And the little girl, to be equally assured, needs to be one of a series of girls, up through the nubile girl with budding breasts to the mature young woman, and finally to the just pregnant, the fully pregnant and the post-parturient and suckling mother. This is what happens in those primitive societies in which the body is hardly covered at all and most of the bodily changes are present to the child's eye. . . . The worried and frightened comparison between the small boy and his father — the only exhibit of maleness that is vouchsafed to him in our society — are not the characteristic features of such an experience.

This is not to say that we should go all the way back to nature, but that occasional exposure to parental nudity

129

and a high school course in sex education are not enough. Our society has made progress since Mead's words were written in 1949. Summer fashions and beachwear have approached the limits of nudity, advanced pregnancy no longer impels a woman to stay out of the public eye, and a nursing mother need no longer retire to the bedroom to feed her baby.

The "unisex" fashions in clothes and social behavior adopted by youth in the past few years might look like a step in the wrong direction, but they can also be seen as a healthy move to tie gender differences more firmly to the basic differences in anatomy rather than to conventional differences in the cut of clothes and hair. The facts that long-haired boys usually sport moustaches, beards, or sideburns and that most jeans-clad girls spurn brassieres and girdles support this view. The children of the "unisex" generation already show signs of being more relaxed about the superficial differences in gender roles than even their young parents.

Nevertheless there are surprisingly many American children today who literally do not know the genital difference between males and females, others who have a great store of misinformation about reproduction to confuse them, and still others who know enough but are so inhibited that they can't talk about it, a milder form of the mutism that afflicted the two hermaphrodite children described in Chapter 4. Small wonder that they grow up clinging desperately to the superficial sex differences, for one must have *something* to cling to, if it's only that "men are helpless in the kitchen," or "women can't drive a nail in straight." Children whose gender schemas are built around the sturdy framework of accurate information about the genital sex differences and their uses can afford more freedom in pursuing their individual bents, and later they can wash dishes or shovel coal, tend children or run for public office, without straining their confidence in themselves as masculine or feminine.

Ideally, parents will unostentatiously allow their children to become acquainted, from infancy on, with the nude appearance of family members, juvenile and adult, in the normal course of dressing, undressing and bathing. Ideally, also, they will acquaint their children from an early age, step by step, with information about where babies come from, and how; they will not be evasive about the function of the penis and vagina in intercourse.

Lack of a simple, untarnished terminology handicaps those who want to be honest with young children about sexual intercourse. The English language has been robbed of the simple, graphic sex words. They've been banned, then sneaked back into common currency as insults and badges of defiance. When overuse wears away these counterfeit meanings, perhaps they can again serve at face value. Meanwhile, instead of straightforward words like "dick," "cunt" and "fuck," there is only a choice between fuzzy euphemisms such as "private parts" and "making love," or clinical terms such as "penis," "vagina" and "copulation," or pomposities such as "male member," "female organs," and "sexual relations." Even in kindergarten, however, a child can understand a story that tells of the swimming race of the sperm, competing for the prize of joining with the egg to start a baby growing — 300 million of them and only one winner. The sperm are pumped out of the penis, the story can explain, and to give them a fair chance at the start of the race, the penis fits into the baby tunnel or birth canal — the vagina — in much the same way as a thumb fits into your mouth, if you suck your thumb. Moreover, it feels good and comforting when two parts of the body are fitted together like that just as a thumb feels comforting to a thumb-sucker, but it is much more exciting than sucking your thumb.

Parents who are at ease with their own sexuality and really enjoy their sex lives are good at being able to recognize their children's sexual curiosity and to provide information in appropriate installments. These parents do not wait for their children's questions in order to answer them honestly, for they know that waiting makes it already too late. Children learn the taboo on sexuality in our society all too soon, and it freezes up their natural inquiries. Parents should be the ones who break the ice.

Parents who are at ease with their own sexuality make the sharing of sexual knowledge always so open within the family that they don't need to prepare a biological lecture for a mother-to-daughter or father-to-son talk on the eve of puberty. The timing of such a talk is too late, and its aim is too narrow, even if a parent is able to deliver it free from distorting embarrassment. Moreover, such talks, like most formal sex education courses (in schools that offer them), are almost invariably limited to the mechanics of reproduction. Useful as information about reproductive processes may be, it is not by itself an adequate foundation for full sexual development. To deal with reproduction and leave out sensuality, eroticism, and love is little help to a preadolescent child who is trying to find out what sex is all about. Human sexuality involves all the senses — touch, taste, sight, smell, and hearing — and the most ecstatic reaches of emotion and sensation. To give the reproductive facts but leave out these elements is to falsify an otherwise accurate recital. This falsification helps to sustain an idiotic but disastrous dichotomy between love and lust, between romance, falling in love, tenderness and devotion on one side, and anything to do with sex organs on the other. "Don't touch your genitals, they're dirty, so save them for the one you're going to love," but "love is so pure, the one you love so sacred, that to even think of using your sex organs with him or her befouls the relationship."

The taboo on sexual terminology has as its counterpart the taboo on pictorial representations of sex. In the mass media, our children have ample access to sex models with the secondary sex characteristics grossly exaggerated, but seldom to honest portrayals of naked human bodies and virtually never to frank depictions of copulation or birth. Children can see people quarreling, fighting, and killing each other, often in ghastly and ingenious ways, even in the television shows and comic strips designed for children. But sexual intercourse? Never. It might, society fears, incite them to go out and do — who knows what? "Monkey see, monkey do" is the false proverbial philosophy that society uses to justify its taboo on sexual pictures. In point of fact, children don't automatically copy everything they see. Consider, for example, that millions of children over hundreds of years have been given detailed, illustrated lessons on crucifixion. Have you ever heard of children rushing home from Sunday school to play crucifixion games? The point is, of course, that the Crucifixion of Christ is presented to children in a moral context. Along with the technique, they learn the moral significance of what happened on that Friday, and even very young children are adept at absorbing moral precepts that are presented to them in a proper context. When it comes to presenting human sexuality, however, our society is hopelessly confused about what the proper moral context is.

The same principles apply to the use of explicit sexual pictures. They can and should be used as part of a child's sex education, but where can parents and teachers find suitable pictures? The sophisticated drawings in a book like Alex Comfort's *The Joy of Sex* (1972) are much too elaborate and fanciful to be useful as a primer, and straightforward photographs are not easy to find. For example, some of the best photographs we've seen are badly reproduced on cheap paper in *The Pictorial Guide to Sexual Intercourse* by Schwenda and Leuchner (1969), which is available (if it still is) only in some of the unsavory "adult" bookshops.

The best time to introduce such pictures is before a child's biological clock has signaled the start of puberty. Prepubertal children are intellectually capable of understanding sex, and their curiosity about life runs high. They will no doubt find these pictures erotically stimulating, but as the novelty wears off they will soon settle down and accept the information in the matter-of-fact way they accept information about other facets of adult life. If their first exposure to pictures of sexual relations between men and women comes after hormonal puberty has begun, the education will still be helpful but their erotic response will be harder for them to manage and they will need more exposure before the pictures cease to arouse it. In short, it takes older children longer to grow bored with such pictures.

A more complicated situation arises when a child happens to observe an adult couple engaged in sexual intercourse. Copulatory privacy is so embedded in our society's sexual taboo that the idea of learning about sexual intercourse by seeing it in real life shocks most people. The fact is, however, that millions of the world's children grow up to be quite normal sexually in families whose members all sleep together in the same living space with sexual intercourse an open secret if it is a secret at all. Sexual intercourse can safely be explained to our children as a game grown-ups play. With a little calm guidance, the experience can be integrated into the child's sex education and serve to reinforce his or her own gender identity/role. But when adults panic, the experience becomes traumatic for all concerned. Even with wise guidance, however, children in a society that cherishes coital privacy must pay a penalty for witnessing sexual intercourse since they must then be burdened with either keeping the experience a secret or being labeled "bad" by less enlightened playmates and their families and possibly by their teachers as well, if they talk about it.

The sexual organs themselves are active from birth. Some normal girl babies have a slight amount of menstrual bleeding for a day or two after they are separated from their mother's hormones, and boy babies get penile erections, sometimes on the day they're born. Babies of both sexes have been known to exercise their bodies and genitals rhythmically so as to achieve spasmodic muscular reactions that resemble sexual climax, and in some cultures it's customary to stroke an infant's genitals as a way of soothing distress or lulling the baby to sleep. Evidence that babies normally experience something very like the pleasure and comfort adults derive from sex is not hard to find. In a social and geographic climate that permits children to go naked, you often see nursing children quite ingenuously and almost absentmindedly fondle their genitals, and the little boys get an erection.

It need hardly be said that punishment for these kinds of activities has a devastating effect on a child's self-image, developing concepts of sensuality, and feelings about close body contact. The baby's psychosexual normalcy depends on the good feeling of joy and security in hugging, cuddling, fondling and skin contact, especially when being fed. Early theorists of child development failed to appreciate the importance of body contact and infantile clinging to normal gender identity differentiation in human beings, and to their psychosexual development in general. The suspicion that these are essential was aroused by studies of children raised in foundling homes where they had been shortchanged in human contact and clinging. Studies of monkeys reared in isolation have brought home the full significance. Year by year, monkey studies have been building up the evidence, and there is now no longer any question that unless a monkey has a mother to cling to in infancy and agemates to play with in early childhood, it cannot copulate normally and reproduce when it grows up.

Monkeys play sexual games with their playmates, rehearsing the crouching, mounting, and thrusting that will later be used in sexual intercourse. They also play at masturbation, and masturbation too is a normal part of human infancy and childhood. In fact all of the sensory and motoric part-functions of lovemaking and sex are intact from early childhood, and if they are eventually to be coordinated and patterned into a functional whole, the child needs a chance to exercise them, just as in other types of development. Newborns, for example, have legs and can make treading motions with them, although it will be some time before they can walk, and babies vocalize long before they can talk. Parents and siblings constantly serve as models for the baby to show how it's done. The baby's treading and vocalizing elicit delighted encouragement, which helps the child learn, and take pleasure and pride in learning, to walk and talk. But in our society, experiments with sexual part-functions are firmly discouraged, and any model of how the part-functions will eventually fit together in copulatory behavior patterns is top secret. Imagine the handicap of trying to learn to walk or talk under such conditions.

A baby boy needs help and reassurance in identifying himself as a boy who will grow up to be a man and help in learning how to do it. He needs to know that his penis is a proud, integral part of what makes him a boy, a promise of his future manhood, and he needs a concept of how he will use his penis to validate his manhood. It's easy for a mother who may adore her baby but despise her husband and his penis to communicate to her infant son in subtle, covert ways a conviction that he would be even more adorable if it weren't for that rather disgusting little appendage on his belly. Anxiously the baby, whose life is so literally in her hands, must seek to wish away the offending member. If such messages are compelling enough in infancy, and are not countered by his father, the baby can be led to reject his penis and his masculinity altogether, heading toward transexualism.

A baby girl needs help and reassurance in identifying herself as a girl who will grow up to be a woman and help in learning how to do it. She needs to know that her vulva is a proud, integral part of what makes her a girl, a promise of her future womanhood, and she needs a concept of how her vagina and the hidden "baby nest" above it will validate her womanhood. It's easy for parents and others to convey in subtle ways the message that there's something vaguely disgusting about a vagina and menstruation; in fact, such messages are built into many cultures and are anything but subtle. The fact that it's women who give birth to all babies, male and female, makes it harder to deflect a girl into differentiating a male gender identity, but it can be done. A parent who wants to use a daughter as a substitute for a wished-for son can, without admitting it even to himself or herself, let the baby girl know unmistakably that the way to the parental love on which her life depends is for her to code her male schema positive. If such messages are compelling enough and are not countered, she can be led to reject her femininity and head for transexualism.

All children need to understand conception and the birth process, particularly the function of the girl's vagina as a "baby canal." If they do not, sooner or later they will have to devise for themselves some explanation of how babies start and how they are delivered. The fanciful conclusions they are likely to reach on their own may be highly entertaining to adults, but can easily distort a child's future sex life. And it is especially important that both boys and girls appreciate the simple fact that conception is a cooperative venture. If a little boy says, as a two-year-old who had watched with fascination the pregnancy of a neighbor and the subsequent arrival of a baby recently did, "I've got babies in *my* tummy," he ventures the statement tentatively and looks to his parents for confirmation. The answer, "No, darling, babies only grow in a mommy's tummy," is honest, but robs the little boy of his rightful sense of participation in this vital process. People almost invariably describe conception as sperm swimming up to fertilize the egg, but in truth it is equally accurate to say that the egg comes down to meet and fertilize the sperm. The answer, "No, darling, not in your tummy, you have babies in your testicles but they grow only in a mommy's tummy," gives the little boy what he is seeking — accurate knowledge of his own future part in creating babies.

Once gender identity differentiates as male or female, one schema is coded positive, the other negative. Confusion thereafter doesn't change this but may affect the sorting of behavior into the two schemas. The sorting process is not very well understood, but it is where some types of homosexuality originate. When a child is old enough to ask questions about sexual behavior, what he or she wants to know is how, when, where, and with whom sex should be explored, and how to behave in matters of peer group curiosity. What a child usually gets may be a spanking, a frown, a blank look, an evasive answer, a biological lecture, or at best a message that adds up to "It's so wonderful you shouldn't have anything to do with it." Such responses quickly teach the child not to expect any useful guidance. While the fact of child sexuality has long since been established, neither the fact nor its significance as a basis of adult sexuality has yet had much impact on social conventions.

Prohibiting sex play doesn't stop it, but does drive it underground, leaving children to grope at each other guiltily in the dark. Prohibiting sex play also leaves parents in the dark about their children's sexual development. Since the mistakes that are made don't usually show up clearly until puberty, and since by then it's hard to trace the errors back to their source in childhood, little has been learned about how to diagnose these problems while there is still time to correct them. To perpetuate this dangerous situation, scientific investigation is also prohibited on the rationale that to study children's sexuality would violate the age of innocence and also, quite paradoxically, that it would stir up in the children the lurking demon of original sin. Scientists who propose such studies are more likely to be threatened with prosecution than funded, so that to date childhood sexuality remains the arcane subject of unconfirmed doctrine, projection and conjecture, while children and those responsible for their welfare are preserved not in innocence but in ignorance.

The fact that there are cultures which encourage children's interest in their genitals and their rehearsals of copulatory behavior, and that these cultures seem to be remarkably free of impotence and other psychosexual disorders that plague our own society, strongly suggests that there are better ways of managing childhood sexuality than trying to squelch it. Their ways may not be ours, but we're hardly likely to find better ways for ourselves by refusing to look for them.

When it comes to the erotic functioning of the most potent of the human sex organs, the brain, our society today leaves education to disk jockeys, poets, novelists, dramatists, folk singers, and the franker autobiographers who, if they get too explicit, are censored. The business of erotic and sexual censorship is so enmeshed in conflicting paradoxes that it confuses the best judicial minds in the land, not to mention the minds of children, adolescents, and parents. Attempts to define obscenity and pornography are often ludicrous.

Somehow in the course of history we have managed to define as obscene the nude human body and the way it is reproduced. When the legal restrictions on portrayal of nudity were eased recently, the compromise arrived at by a United States court was pathetic. The majesty of the law decreed that in this greatest, most powerful country on earth, a naked man and woman together may be publicly portrayed only if the man's penis is flaccid and impotent!

As to what constitutes pornography, the high courts have painted themselves into an odd corner by defining it as that which appeals to prurient interest. Since prurient means itchy, and an interest in sex is perfectly normal, that definition is no help. The itchiness comes not from what you see but from the sense of wrongdoing you get from taking a sneaky peek at what you've been indoctrinated to believe you shouldn't look at. There won't be any sensible answers until the courts and the public accept a more realistic view of what pornography can and cannot do. Pornography will not turn a child into a sex degenerate, a sex maniac, or even a picture freak, nor does pornography broaden the appetites of a deviant at any age. Vendors of pornography know very well that their financial success depends on catering to the established tastes of their regular customers. The people who keep the porn shops in business don't browse around; they come in for their own kind of thing and they don't want any other kind. The tourist trade is fly-by-night and soon exhausts itself.

Honest pornography might, however, help to prevent twists in sexual development. When Denmark lifted all legal restrictions on pornography in 1969, the upsurge in sex crimes which many had confidently predicted failed to materialize. In fact, Denmark's sex crime rate plummeted. Most notable was a prompt and sharp decline in the incidence of child molestation. No doubt there are better ways than pornography to satisfy the itch of normal curiosity about sex, but leaving children in a morass of ignorance about a significant aspect of their being is hardly one of them, nor is it any help to them in sorting out gender behavior. Consider the pathology you would have to expect in a society that prescribed secret eating, banned cookbooks and pictures of food, and pretended that children never eat at all.

Instead of wringing hands over the incidence of sexual deviation and sex crimes, our society would do better to support research on how sexuality develops. If we knew more about how sexuality normally evolves, and if our children were encouraged to be open and inquiring instead of secretive about their sexual feelings, discrepancies could be identified and often corrected before they could do any permanent harm. As it is, we routinely check children's height, weight, posture, physical coordination, eyesight, and so forth, but we have no way of checking on their erotic development. We wouldn't know what to look for if we did, and have only a pitifully limited knowledge of corrective measures to apply when we suspect things are going awry.

Provided you were lucky and nothing went awry, you emerged from infancy with a sense of goodness in body contact as a foundation for genuinely erotic experience later, and for a masculine or feminine differentiation of gender identity/role. Identification and complementation both fell into place as you differentiated your two sex schemas, and you grew secure in yourself and secure in your sexual anatomy.

The emphasis on identification and the neglect of complementation in most theories of child development and in the studies based on them has obscured the significance of your other-sex schema. It did not, however, wither away as did the other-sex wolffian or mullerian structures. Your other-sex schema serves as your guide to behavior that is not appropriate for you, but *is* appropriate for the other sex. It not only tells you negatives — how not to think, feel and behave — but also what to expect of the other sex, and so frames your perception of, and influences your reaction to, members of the other sex. You might say that the positive coding of your same-sex schema puts green lights in some behavior lanes while the negative coding of your other-sex schema puts red lights in other lanes both to warn you off and to tell you where the other traffic is going.

An intelligent and insightful psychiatrist whose wife is a physician provided a good illustration of how the other-sex schema operates when he recently addressed a gender identity conference. He described the eminently fair division of domestic duties he and his wife had worked out and lovingly put into practice, but then he confessed, "And I hate it!" He blamed this on his lack of training and experience in housework and child care. But would lack of training and experience have made him hate golf, for example, if he took it up at the same age? He might have blamed his prenatal hormone mix for raising the threshold of his response to the young, but that couldn't be the answer either, for he had already surmounted that threshold. What he overlooked is that housework and child care are lodged firmly in his other-sex schema and coded negative for him. Running the red lights will no doubt continue to make him acutely uncomfortable unless he can decode these activities.

Looking at the schemas in this way may help others to understand the problems of transexuals. As long as society makes them follow the traffic pattern for their anatomy and label, they are under the strain of constantly running lights that their gender identity insists are red. If they change labels and anatomy in maturity, as Cowell and others have done, there is the relief of being able to go with their own green lights, but it takes a while for them to adjust all their reflexes and interact smoothly. Transsexuals who change their label to match their gender identity soon fit comfortably into the traffic pattern; if not their first nature, it quickly becomes second nature to them. Transvestites who switch back and forth get the experience of interacting in both roles and so can move easily in conventional traffic under either label, up to the point where genital anatomy comes into play.

In short, if you're a man you use your female schema to anticipate the behavior of girls and women and as a guide to how you will react to them as a male. If you're a woman you use your male schema to anticipate the behavior of boys and men and as a guide to how you will respond to them reciprocally as a woman.

You can find evidence of this complementary function of your other-sex schema by looking for the threads of consistency in your responses to members of the opposite sex. There are some that persist regardless of which particular member of the opposite sex you may be responding to at the moment. There are, for example, women who defer to the wisdom of men in, say, financial matters. Since financial astuteness is a feature of her male schema, such a woman automatically expects it in every man and finds it hard to reject a man's advice about money even if the man offering it is patently unsuccessful in managing his own finances. There are men who automatically heed the voice of a woman's — any woman's — intuition, and so on. Your other-sex schema is a lens through which you perceive the members of the opposite sex. So is your same-sex schema, but there's less chance of distortion in this case since the only question with members of your own sex is the extent of identification. You don't have to bother with complementation, unless, of course, there is enough age or status difference to oblige you to complement rather than simply to identify.

A misogynist man and a man-hating woman are prisoners of their other-sex schemas. H. L. Mencken, an astute observer of his fellow men, revealed the blinkers his female schema put on his perception of women when he wrote, "Love is the delusion that one woman differs from another." In *My Fair Lady*, Professor Higgins describes his male and female schemas in song. "Why can't a woman be more like a man?" he asks plaintively. The song makes it clear he has completely failed to notice that the woman he's in love with, and has been working with closely for half a year, is no more like the picture of her he sees through his female schema than he himself resembles the picture of himself drawn by his male schema.

Professor Higgins's eyes are opened to give the plot a happy ending, but some of the students at medical school — or at any other professional school, for that matter — provide a sad real-life example of the limitations a gender schema can impose. You'd think the boys would look for dates among the girls in their classes, girls who share their interests and ambitions and understand their problems. It would certainly be more convenient for them, if nothing else, to make and keep dates with girl medical students. But since most of the boys have nothing in their gender schemas that tells them how to interact with girls who are their intellectual and professional equals, they drift into the traditional relationships with nurses, women technicians, and girls from other colleges. The girl medical students are even worse off; they don't know how to respond to their male classmates either, and there haven't been enough girl medical students to give them traditional relationships to fall back on.

Such limitations are not confined to students. In America today, a normally heterosexual man who is a dancer, secretary, or househusband by vocation is likely to be pretty lonely. Since almost everybody has these vocations firmly locked into their female schemas, their male schemas give them no basis on which to interact with him. One way out is to assume that he's bisexual or homosexual, but unless the assumption happens to be true, any approach to him on this basis only leads to further misunderstandings. The only way most people can interact with him is either to decode these vocations and put them in their human schema, which, if they can do it at all, may require considerable effort, or to ignore the fact that he's a male and interact with him as human but sexless, which is also pretty hard for most people. Unless there's a strong reason to the contrary, few will take the trouble. The result is that most men are effectively barred from some vocations, whatever their tastes and talents for them. Similar barriers, long existing against women in almost all professions and a great many other vocations, have slowly begun to break down.

There's also the situation of a Jane Smith who marries a John Jones but continues to use her maiden name. She grew up as Jane Smith, the name is embedded in her sense of herself as a person — why should she throw it away when she marries? There's a certain irony in her legal position. The law now holds her responsible as a citizen in her own right. Nevertheless, legally, in most jurisdictions, she is Mrs. Jones. Yet if someone introduces her as

Jones's mistress, which is what Mrs. Jones literally means, she can sue for slander.

Aside from possible legal complications and besides incurring the suspicion of tradesmen, wolves, and gossipy neighbors who suspect she's up to something, Jane will suffer social penalties simply because most people's female schemas don't tell them how to interact with a wife who doesn't use her husband's name. Her friends and family, who call her "Jane" anyway, will no doubt continue to interact with her as before, but they will be inclined to stutter awkwardly when called upon to introduce her. Women who are dissatisfied with the female stereotype will be interested, but most men and many women will simply turn away. Although they might be happy to make friends with her as either Miss Smith or Mrs. Jones, they don't have an easy approach to a Jane Smith-with-unidentified-husband, and the extra effort needed to find a new approach can easily nip potential friendships in the bud. It remains to be seen if the new form, Ms., will smooth over this situation.

If our Jane, unwilling to be thus cut off from potential male acquaintances, figures out what the problem is, she might expand her own female schema to allow herself to make all the initial overtures of friendship to the men she meets. Alas, this won't solve her problem. To respond to her, a conventional man would then not only have to alter his female schema to accept a married woman who uses her own name, he would also have to disregard his own male schema's prescription that men take the initiative in encounters with women. Furthermore, her unconventionally friendly overtures will most likely be interpreted as an invitation to a sexual relationship, whether meant that way or not.

147

Another nuisance for Jane is that hardly a day will pass without the solicitous inquiry "Is that Miss or Mrs.?" when she gives her name. Ninety-nine times out of a hundred, the person who asks doesn't care in the least whether Jane is married or not, or whom she might be married to, but whatever Jane answers is wrong. If she says "Miss," she implies that she is not married, but neither is she Mrs. Jane Smith. If she's Mrs. anything, it's Jones, and what's the point of hanging onto her own name and then giving the impression that it's not her name at all but her husband's?

Although not very pressing, Jane's dilemmas illustrate how hard it is to decode even an unimportant bit of behavior as long as the cultural stereotype codes it firmly. Cultural stereotypes were the matrix in which your gender schemas took shape in childhood. You can recode or decode behavior that is not deeply embedded in your gender identity/role, and society can modify the cultural stereotypes as it has been doing at an accelerating rate in recent years. If the alterations match up, interaction between you and society goes smoothly, but when they clash, your sense of identity gets the impact. Those whose gender schemas are based firmly on the genital differences and reproductive functions can afford to keep the rest of their schemas flexible enough to buffer such collisions. They are the ones who can either resist stereotype pressures or take advantage of stereotype relaxation as they choose, and do so without damage to their sense of identity, expressing their masculinity or femininity in whatever ways give them the most pleasure and satisfaction. They are secure because there is little likelihood that genital and reproductive sex differences will change for us, our children or our grandchildren — entertaining science fiction

inspired by biological engineering research notwithstanding.

Most of these science fiction projections are still far-out
fairy tales. When it comes to the more likely possibilities
— predetermination of the sex of offspring and ovum
transplants — there is reason to believe that even if they
became entirely feasible tomorrow, they would have far
less impact than the prophets of doom predict. As noted in
Chapter 2, it may soon be possible to choose the sex of
your next child, but would you if you could? There's no
sure way of predicting how popular a new technology will
be or what effect it will have until it becomes available, of
course, but an analysis of the 1970 National Fertility
Study (Westoff and Rindfuss, 1974), which was sup-
ported by the National Institutes of Health, indicates that
among the nearly six thousand married women inter-
viewed, almost half (47 percent) were against the idea of
making such a choice even if a safe, reliable, easy method
were found, and another 15 percent were neutral about it.
The main preference that emerged from the analysis was
for the first-born to be a boy, which might produce a wave
of male births if the technology suddenly became available and were widely adopted by newlyweds, but since
there was an almost equally consistent preference for the
second child to be a girl if the first one is a boy, the male-
female birth ratio would in all probability quickly settle
back to the present 105 to 100. About the only lasting
change indicated by the survey would be a drop in the
number of families with several children all of the same
sex and that, of course, would make no difference in the
ratio of boys to girls outside of those families.

Other projected techniques would have even less impact on male-female relationships in the foreseeable

future. It's true that fertilized eggs have already been successfully transplanted from the uterus of one female animal to the uterus of a foster mother of the same species who gestated and delivered the offspring. This technique will probably be adapted for humans and used to enable young women who have a uterus but no ovaries or defective ovaries to achieve motherhood, including XO women and those whose ovaries have had to be surgically removed. It would also have value for women who are known carriers of defective genes, since it would allow them to experience pregnancy without the risk of transmitting the defect, just as couples whose male partner cannot provide sperm or has defective sperm can now avail themselves of healthy sperm from a sperm-bank donor by artificial insemination.

Then there is a somewhat similar technique for women whose ovaries and uterus are normal but whose fertilized egg does not implant in the uterus, which it must do to survive. An egg can be taken from the woman, fertilized in a test tube with her husband's sperm, and then implanted securely in her uterus. In at least three known instances, the mother has carried on through an otherwise normal pregnancy and delivered a normal child.

If a harmless way to suppress the body's immune reaction that rejects foreign tissues is discovered, it may well be possible to transplant an entire uterus. Since the uterus does not depend on nerve connections to function as an incubator, women who have no uterus, and even men, could be equipped for gestation. If that should become possible, male-to-female transexuals who long for motherhood will no doubt bid for the uteruses of the female-to-male transexuals who now gladly give them up, but there are hardly enough prospective customers to make a dent in the sexual mores.

While these developments will make an enormous difference to those who use them, the point here is that there are far too few potential beneficiaries to have any effect whatever on the way the human race propagates itself. A technique that might possibly influence the human pattern of nurturing children is on the more distant horizon. Prenatal tinkering with the sex hormones of rat embryos has produced adult male rats that lactate. Nonetheless, even if the technique is perfected for humans, how many prospective parents would undergo such risky manipulations in order to equip their sons for wet-nursing?

Techniques that really could change the pattern of human reproduction are much too far out even in science fiction to be taken seriously in any consideration of what a child needs for healthy psychosexual development. There's the proposition that human parents could be spared the rigors of pregnancy and parturition by having their fertilized egg implanted in a female chimpanzee. If hormonally prepared for pregnancy, the slave chimpanzee would serve as an incubator. Beyond that lies cloning. According to cloning theory, a human egg with its nucleus microscopically extracted and replaced with a single cell from your skin or other tissue would develop into an individual more like you than an identical twin. That fictional person, too, could be incubated in a slave chimpanzee.

Fascinating as it may be to speculate on what would happen to gender identity if man and woman should no longer need each other in order to propagate, such speculation is no help to children in differentiating a gender identity/role and schemas that will serve them in the real world. The best insurance of emotional security we can give them is to help them base their gender schemas firmly on the genital and reproductive differences between males and females, and to keep the remaining sex-coded behavior patterns in the flexible part of their schemas so that the behavior can be recoded or decoded if need be without shaking their sense of identity.

6.   Adolescence

P UBERTY IS THE TIME when the physical differences between the sexes blossom out in three-dimensional
glory. It looks like the most obvious turning point of all
the forks on the road to manhood or womanhood. Psychologically and behaviorally, however, it is a time of revelation, not a turning point. Puberty guns the motors of
growth, sex differentiation, and sex drive, but it does not
change the course set in childhood. Any errors of direction that show up at puberty were programmed in long
before.

Resigned parents and teachers have come to accept
emotional storms as an inevitable feature of adolescence.
It may surprise many to learn that there are plenty of
youngsters, even some American youngsters, who sail

153

through their teens at a lively but steady pace. Why, then, is it so difficult for so many?

There is, of course, the adolescent's need to establish independence of parents, and there are the hormonal surges, growth spurt, and concomitant body changes initiated by puberty. While these may account for some teenage heavy weather, for most of the answer one must look to the kind of preparation for sexual maturity our society prescribes. Equanimity at puberty depends on confidence and pride built up during childhood.

People often think of puberty as a single event — a boy's first wet dream, a girl's first menstrual period. Actually, puberty isn't something that happens overnight, but a complex, quiet progression stretching out over about four years. One's first ejaculation or first menstrual period is an obvious climactic event of puberty, but only one of a long series of events.

There is considerable latitude in the age at which puberty begins. What starts the process is a biological clock in the old cortex or the limbic system of the brain. Biological clocks have been defined by Curt Paul Richter (1965), who has made a lifelong study of them and gave them that name, as "inherent timing devices that function quite independently of external events, and to a large extent of internal events." They start and stop the stages of your development, control your autonomic functions, and regulate the biological cycles, of which menstruation is the easiest to recognize.

Not much is known about the biological clock of puberty. It is probably located in the brain cells of your hypothalamus. When the timer signaled puberty, the hypothalamus passed the word to the pituitary. The pituitary, the strawboss of the hormone-producing glands, then stepped up its production of gonadotropic hormones, which spurred your gonads — testicles or ovaries — to increase their sex hormone output from a trickle to a flood.

There's no way yet to pinpoint just when the puberty timer goes off, but experimental evidence indicates that in the United States today, the gonadotropin level starts a rapid rise between the ages of nine and ten. A girl's breasts typically bud around the age of eleven, with first menstruation at twelve or thirteen. A boy's scrotum and testicles usually start to enlarge at age twelve, with first ejaculation at thirteen or fourteen. If these developments took place when you were a year or two older or younger than these ages, you were in the normal bracket.

The biological clock of puberty is not rigidly synchronized with chronological age. Occasionally a child enters puberty at four or five years of age, or even younger. A brain lesion can trip the timer early, but in most of these children there is no sign of brain abnormality. Puberty can also be delayed, perhaps indefinitely, by a variety of conditions or for no apparent reason at all. If you or your child should reach the age of fifteen without showing signs of puberty, however, you would be wise to seek a medical opinion.

A most intriguing mystery about the timing of perfectly normal puberty was discovered not so long ago. As noted in Chapter 1, something has been pushing the biological clock of puberty ahead at the rate of four months every ten years for more than a century. In 1962, J. W. Tanner of London published a chart based on records preserved in Europe and the United States showing a progressive decrease in the average age of first menstruation from over seventeen in 1833 to less than

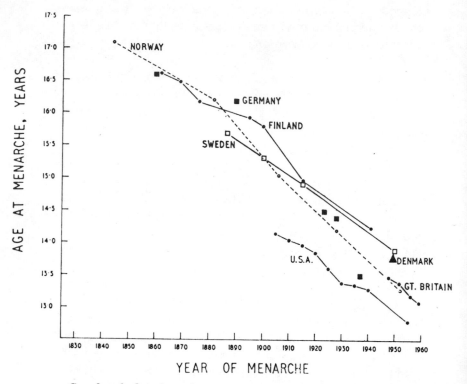

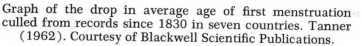

YEAR OF MENARCHE

Graph of the drop in average age of first menstruation culled from records since 1830 in seven countries. Tanner (1962). Courtesy of Blackwell Scientific Publications.

thirteen today (see Figure 1 above). Recently gathered statistics show that this downward trend is worldwide.

Various explanations have been offered, including the fanciful suggestion that the trend began with the invention of the bicycle, which allowed the ordinary people to go courting farther away and so cross-breed with people of other towns and villages. A somewhat more plausible

156

theory ties the drop to a change in food supply and diet following the Napoleonic wars. This theory draws support from the fact that nutrition affects weight, and weight seems to influence the onset of menstruation. Another possible explanation is that more powerful artificial illumination — first the kerosene lamp and then the electric light — is a factor, since light stimulates the pineal gland, which in turn influences hormone production.

In his experiments with mice, John Vandenbergh (1974), in North Carolina, found that diet and the presence or absence of male mice and other female mice, or even just their odor, affect the age at which young females enter upon their first estrus. There are, of course, significant differences between puberty in humans and in mice, and in the kinds of experimenting that can be done with each, but this work led Vandenbergh to the conclusion that "the mean age of menarche may represent the summation of a host of interacting factors such as diet, medical care, and social stimuli." Among the social factors Vandenbergh thinks especially worth considering are contacts with peers, parents, and strangers, and exposure to television and movies. No matter what has been causing the drop, however, adults trying to bridge the generation gap with efforts that start from "When I was your age" would do well to keep the trend firmly in mind.

The surge of sex hormones that initiates puberty kicks off a spurt of growth in the body generally, as well as in the sex organs. Pubic fuzz becomes wiry hair, then axillary hair starts to grow in the armpits. In girls, the breasts begin to bud, the pelvic bones start to spread so there will be room for a baby to pass through, and subcutaneous fat starts collecting in a pattern that rounds the body. In boys, the larynx enlarges into an Adam's apple that deepens the voice, fitfully at first, muscles and bones grow heftier, and eventually facial hair starts a beard.

The hormones that direct these activities do not change the direction of gender identity or the way the schemas are coded. They activate what is there by lowering the barriers to all the lanes of adult sexual behavior, and particularly those of the subjective feelings of eroticism. Both boys and girls discover the ability to fall in love, a heady experience for which the English language has no single word.

The ability to fall passionately in love is the most spectacular behavioral feature of adolescence. There are plenty of scientists who don't hesitate to study the triggers to mating behavior and the pair-bonding of other species, but who scoff at the suggestion that human falling in love could or should be investigated scientifically. They are mistaken, because human falling in love is as much an identifiable phenomenon as the pair-bonding of other species. It can be studied scientifically, and because of its significance — amply attested to by history and by the most enduring of the myths, legends, fairy tales, classics, dramas, and especially poems of all human cultures — it should be. Children often play at falling in love along with their other adult role rehearsals. Whether they come close to the real thing or not is a question that will only be answered by further investigation. It's also normal for children to hero-worship and develop crushes on older children or adults, but these behaviors are fairly easy to distinguish from falling in love. The kind of desperate dependence on an older person some children and adolescents exhibit can be mistaken for falling in love, but it is a pathological condition that probably stems from a deficit of early clinging and cuddling.

Although the ability to fall in love is normally achieved · during the course of puberty, there is evidence that it is governed by a different biological clock. Early puberty does not mean early achievement of the ability to fall in love. Children who reach puberty at four or five years of age or even younger may have wet dreams and masturbation fantasies earlier than other children, but they don't fall in love any earlier. A few children enter puberty before age six, and among those followed in the Psychohormonal Research Unit, the youngest to have fallen genuinely in love were a boy of twelve and a girl of ten, which is not much younger than some of those who reach puberty at the normal ages.

The ability to fall in love is sometimes delayed until long after hormonal puberty. Such late blooming is not related to low hormone levels. It can be due to individual variation in the pace of achieving psychological maturity, to lack of an opportunity to fall in love, or to cultural prescription, as in Red China today where people are adjured to postpone romance and marriage until their late twenties. In some people, however, the ability to fall in love is so weak, or the inhibiting circumstances so strong, that the ability never manifests itself. There are otherwise normal adults who have never fallen in love.

The phenomenon itself is a familiar one. Falling in love is a state characterized by intense preoccupation with the loved one. His or her every feature becomes a source of minor raptures. There is an urgent need to be close to, a yearning to touch and fondle, the loved one, although the expression of these yearnings may be inhibited by moral

159

code, cultural prescription, or circumstance. Reciprocation intensifies the phenomenon.

Falling in love inspires a jealous protectiveness that brooks no competitor. It is monogamous to the extent that it excludes the possibility of simultaneous falling in love with another person, although not the possibility of having sexual relations with another or others.

Falling in love is not a one-time thing; the experience can be repeated again and again. Onset may be sudden or gradual. It's quite possible to fall in love at first sight, or at a distance.

The phenomenon may last only an hour or two or for months, but the maximum duration of the acute phase of a normal falling in love experience is probably no more than two years at the outside. Nature's obvious purpose in designing the falling in love syndrome was to draw the human male and female together as soon as their sex organs matured for reproduction, and keep them together long enough to insure the next generation. As are nature's other designs for perpetuating the various species, this one is wasteful. Falling in love absorbs so much of the time and energy of those involved and so powerfully diverts their attention from other pursuits that the young might not be cared for if it lasted indefinitely. If unrequited, it may persist, but "carrying the torch" soon becomes pathological. Those who can't recover from a broken heart without going through a serious bereavement syndrome aren't lovesick, they're just plain sick. Normal falling in love either passes off completely or resolves into a calm, steady love with, or perhaps without, continuing sexual attraction. Nature's purpose is to replace the two-way bond with a steadier three-way bond that includes father, mother, and child.

There is no better way to establish this three-way bond than by means of prepared or natural childbirth, as anyone who has assisted in a delivery — or even seen a movie of one — will know. The father trains as a coach and is present at the delivery, ready to touch and hold his newborn baby. The mother remains conscious throughout, actively helping to expel the baby, and able to reach down and hold it in her arms as soon as it has safely emerged.

The falling in love archetypes in our culture are the undiscriminatingly seducing Don Juan at one extreme and at the other the ever-faithful wife, Penelope, holding her suitors at bay through the long years against Odysseus's improbable return. Woman-chasers and nymphomaniacs are people who can neither sustain their falling in love reaction for more than a few hours or days nor resolve it into something more permanent, and so must constantly seek new stimuli. Old faithfuls are the torch-carriers who can't let go of a single stimulus, even a painful one. They are often schizoid or schizophrenic people who either can't bring themselves to declare their love, or if they do declare it, can never accept loss of or rejection by the loved one, even when they are victimized. Where you fit on the scale between these extremes is the result of interaction among many factors, notably your temperament, physical make-up, and experience, and the conventions of your culture.

In a study of the way people react to pain, Asenath Petrie (1967) of Harvard classified her subjects as augmenters and diminishers. In the general sense, diminishers are those whose experiences fade quickly. They need constant repetition in order to make sure of having experienced anything at all. Augmenters are those whose experiences reverberate and expand in memory. Having once experienced something, it haunts them. They can't exorcise it. This classification may help to explain the differences in duration of the falling in love response. Perhaps the way you store your memories is part of the interaction that determines the pattern of your falling in love.

Any visual feature of the human body can serve as a trigger for the falling in love response. A symbol — photograph, drawing, or mental picture — can sometimes suffice. The face is often the focal point but hips, torso, chest, and legs are also potent stimuli and, as in the Gay Nineties, ankles.

Where complete nudity is the rule, as it was among the Australian aborigines for example, motions and gestures with erotic implications must substitute. In societies that favor covering the body completely, the part dèemed most alluring can be exposed with devastating effect, or hidden to discourage the falling in love response. The woman who flicks her veil aside for an instant in a strictly orthodox Moslem country may transmit a more powerful erotic signal than the girl who waltzes down Broadway in a halter and miniskirt.

When puberty reveals the particular kind of stimulus that arouses your erotic response it can come as a jolt, especially if what turns you on is not what song and story had led you to expect would do so. Such jolts hit boys much harder than girls. Since vivid, explicit sex dreams don't usually come to girls until after they've had real-life sexual experiences, a girl can arrive gradually at a realization of what sort of stimulus arouses her and how she responds, but a boy is self-presented at puberty with nature's own pornography show in his dreams, the aptly called wet dreams he is powerless to censor. No act of will can change his dream imagery. He must face his truth, whatever it has become, all at once as he enters adolescence.

The spontaneous appearance at puberty of sex dreaming — wet dreaming — independent of sexual experience may be programmed into the brain pathways by prenatal male sex hormones, another manifestation of the Adam principle. Some support for this hypothesis comes from a gonadally male girl born with hermaphroditic sex organs. When she embarked upon a masculinizing puberty, she had sex dreams (although the imagery was suitably feminine) and after her testicles were removed and hormonal replacement with female hormones begun, the sex dreaming ceased.

Whatever the determining factor may be, there is ample evidence that a sexual response is usually more readily initiated by visual stimuli in males and by tactile stimuli in females. The male-female difference in response to a sexy picture has been aphoristically described as the difference between "I want to have" and "I want to be." When viewing an erotic movie, for example, men tend to complement themselves to the opposite sex, whereas women tend to identify with their own sex.

Both men and women find erotic stimulation in sexy films, but a man is likely to see the pictured female as a sex object, take her off the screen in his imagination, and fantasize intercourse with her on the spot. A woman is more likely to identify with the female actress and build her erotic excitement into a fantasy of being in the picture herself, the object of male attention, using the experience in her imagination to enlarge her repertory of sexual skills so that she herself will be more irresistible to her partner, or to the next man who catches her romantic fancy. The romantic overture to the embrace of the partner is important to her. Pinup girls and "feelthy" pictures are the staple of the barbershop and GI barracks, but in the beauty shop and WAC barracks, it's the "confessions" magazine that is the real pornography. Legislatures solemnly framing laws against pornography never think of including a ban on the confession-type magazines because the men who dominate the lawmaking process have never bothered to find out what constitutes pornography for women.

Perhaps, after all, this difference comes down to a question of nature's economics. A woman, with a fixed number of ova to last her a lifetime, typically wants to feel a man close to her, touching her, before she responds erotically. A man, who prodigally generates sperm to order, can afford to pursue a fainter prospect. The symbol — vision, photograph, dream or memory — is enough to set the blood racing to his penis.

Because erotic preferences usually reveal themselves at puberty, it is often assumed that they were instilled by a first sexual experience at that time, or caught from exposure to erotic pictures, books, or films, an assumption that is responsible for much of today's judicial panic about pornography. On the contrary, each person's turn-on has rather fixed boundaries which are set before puberty. Whether the boundaries are orthodox or unorthodox, conventional or unconventional, they were established in childhood as part of the differentiation of gender identity, by the coding of the schemas, and by any quirks or oddities that were incorporated into the schemas. Boundaries may first show themselves at puberty, but they are not set in puberty, and they don't change much, at puberty or later. Their relative unchangeability helps to explain such phenomena as why a second spouse so often resembles the first. Their persistence also explains why adult obligative homosexuals can be fond of and behave affectionately toward a member of the other sex, especially if the other is older, but can never fall in love with her or him. Tales of sex degenerates who go from one form of depravity to another, sampling everything, are only fiction; even so-called sex degenerates stick to their particular preferences.

The reassuring truth is that it's impossible to influence or train any teenager selected at random to be a sadist, a fetishist, a peeping tom or whatever else you name. Nor can a few exposures to homosexuality in early adolescence create an appetite for more and more so that they turn the youngster into a permanent homosexual (Money, 1973b). The worst a homosexual experience can do toward making an adolescent homosexual is to whet a dormant appetite that had already been created in childhood. For proof there are the societies that prescribe a period of homosexuality for adolescent boys as a standard part of the growing-up process. Examples are the Batak people of Lake Toba in northern Sumatra and until recently the Marind Amin people of southern New Guinea (Money and Ehrhardt, 1972). In these cultures, which have endured successfully for centuries, the homosexual period is followed by heterosexual marriage. Their marriages are far more stable than in our own society, and furthermore, researchers could find no adult obligative homosexuals in either culture.

If the kind of stimulus that arouses your erotic feelings and the kind of sexual behavior it inspires you to came as a pubertal surprise, the surprise was prepared in the psychosexual program laid down during your early years.

For those who at puberty feel shocked or guilty when they learn what turns them on and how they respond, it's too late to do too much about it. The only hope of changing erotic stimulus-response patterns at or after puberty lies in major, long-term, therapeutic reeducation, and it is not a very strong hope.

Clues to a child's developing sexual preferences can be found in the imagery of masturbation fantasies and the stories children make up about sex. Our society ruthlessly forces children to hide such clues from their parents and disguise them to themselves so that it's hard to recognize them, even for a trained therapist who braves society to look for them.

Then, when puberty drives the erotic preferences into a youngster's full awareness, he or she gets no help in assessing them. After burdening them as children with a load of shame and guilt, the official attitude has long been to keep adolescents in ignorance, confining sex education, if any, to the mechanics of reproduction. How is a youngster to know if an occasional homosexual impulse means that he or she is any "queerer" than everyone else? Or whether cruelty in erotic dreams represents a normal kind of love fighting or sadism? If it's an object that stimulates a boy's or girl's erotic feelings, is the object a fetish or a symbol? Textbooks, films, and courses on anatomy and reproduction are now available to many teenagers, but none on love play and sexual intercourse. Adolescents need from society sex education that includes the erotic, gymnastic and love aspects of sex as well as the reproductive aspects. About their only hope of getting it, outside of trial and often painful error, is to luck onto a counselor who is both wise and honest or one of the few really useful books on the subject. Parents and teachers seldom suspect that the "difficult" behavior they expect as a matter of course in their adolescent charges may originate in perplexity over the clash between conventional imagery and the erotic imagery that emerges in puberty — perplexity that a reassuring word from a sympathetic adult could often dispel.

Schooled not to ask questions about sex, most youngsters feel that their parents and teachers are the last people they can turn to for advice. The adult world has erected "no trespassing without a marriage license" barriers around sexuality. When the hormones of puberty rev up the sexual motors and speed the youngster toward the barriers, the adult world is prepared to watch with tolerant amusement his or her awkward attempts at compromise to avoid collision, and to persecute those who crash, but not to offer much help Psychological counseling, when it is available, still has a long way to go, first to earn and then to win the confidence of teenagers. Seldom can they rely on their agemates, since few teenagers can afford the fearful risk of being labeled "different." So agonies must be suffered in silence.

Though painfully slow in coming, there are signs of a break in this policy of isolation. Honest sex education courses and movies that deal with love relationships and erotic recreation, as well as physiology, are filtering down from college to high school, and will eventually move down into grammar school, where they can do the most good.

Another hopeful sign is the minor revolution in children's literature now taking place, all but unnoticed. The *Siecus Report* of November 1972 carried an article by Lorna Flynn (1972) called "The Hardy Boys Didn't Have Wet Dreams." It brings the good news that fiction for preteeners and teenagers is beginning to offer the kind of reality these age groups need and which they cannot get from either the classics or adult fiction, or from the children's books of only a few short years ago.

"Today's fictional twelve-year-old girls begin to menstruate," Lorna Flynn reports. Harriet, a spy in *The Long Secret* by Louise Fitzhugh, gets her period and goes right on trying to solve her mystery. Following the lead of the award-winning book by John Donovan, *I'll Get There, It Better Be Worth the Trip*, several other authors have dealt openly with teenage homosexual experiences. In Barbra Wersba's novel *Run Softly, Go Fast*, ignorance leads adults to panic out of all proportion over a brief homosexual experience of a kind familiar to many adolescents. Thirteen-year-old Tony in *Then Again, Maybe I Won't*, by Judith Blume, spends his evenings watching the girl next door undress, and his first wet dream centers around her. All this is a far cry from the juvenile fiction of even the recent past.

The generation gap is often blamed on the fact that acceleration in the rate of technological change makes the training and experience adults have accumulated over the years obsolete so quickly. More than ever before, it's true that young people today have fewer economic skills to learn by watching and listening to their elders. Perhaps of greater significance is the widening spread between the age at which young people are expected to assume adult economic responsibilities — which has been going steadily up — and the age at which they attain sexual maturity, which we now know has been going steadily down for more than a century. Economic maturity, which once often preceded, then coincided with, sexual maturity, now follows it by some years.

However practical it may once have been to insist that young people make a good start toward achieving their economic goals before beginning their sex lives, the increasing spread between coming of age sexually and coming of age economically makes it less than practical today. As long as sex routinely led to more children to be cared for and more mouths to be fed, society had good reason to insist that sexual independence wait for economic and social independence, whatever the cost to the individual. Now that reliable contraception is within the reach of all, however, economic and societal sense lie in demanding only that people who are not prepared to assume adult responsibility as parents practice contraception, not that they abjure sexual activity.

Looking back, one can see why this change caught society unaware. Hard as it may be to realize, until not so long ago there was no recognized "adolescent age," no teenage group with its own customs and its own acknowledged problems, sexual or any other kind. Society considered your great-grandfather — who may well have left school to start earning a living about the time he reached puberty — a child until he put on long pants and became a man. The law called him an infant until he was twenty-one. Your grandmother was regarded as a child until she put up her hair and started looking around for a husband. Adolescence was a brief transition period until earlier puberty and later economic and social maturity stretched it into a stage of life.

Things came to a head in the 1960s when the adolescent population suddenly ballooned out of all proportion to the rest of the population, thanks to the post–World War II baby boom. In 1970 there were almost thirteen million more fourteen-to-twenty-four-year-olds in the

United States than there had been in 1960. While the total U.S. population was growing by some 13 percent during that decade, the fourteen-to-twenty-four subgroup grew by a staggering 46 percent. Daniel Moynihan, an urban affairs expert, called the shift an absolutely unprecedented phenomenon, and predicted that it will never happen again. In an article published by the *Washington Post* on July 29, 1973, he wrote: "Well, it's over. That time is past. We are going through a period now when we are going to have a profound change in almost all of our politics, almost all of our social relationships, because that period is behind us."

There are a few signs that the age of puberty is beginning to level off, and the 1960s teenage bulge that dramatized the need to adjust gender stereotypes for a more protracted adolescence has receded, but adolescence has become and remains a stage of life. Its needs have scarcely been met. Earlier dating, a more permissive attitude toward premarital sex, and provision for married students represent efforts to ease the strain, but far more radical adjustments will have to be made before adolescence becomes adequate preparation for sexual maturity in today's world.

How people select their sex partners from among those available to them is a never-failing source of wonderment to all. Commonly referred to as matters of the heart, dating and mating are in fact matters of the brain and hormones, best understood in the light of their evolutionary development.

To begin with, bisexual reproduction is only one of the ways in which species propagate themselves. The species that reproduce by cloning don't have the problems of pairing. Paramecia, green aphids and some other species alternate between simple division and bisexual reproduction. Some bisexual species avoid pairing problems by supplying each individual with both male and female elements. Plants of this type may pollinate either themselves or each other, and in some lowly animal species like earthworms, each individual develops both male and female organs to functional maturity. An earthworm can reproduce alone or copulate with another earthworm to fertilize and be fertilized at the same time.

In other species, notably some kinds of fish, the individuals function as male at one stage of their lives, female at another. As described in Chapter 3, experimenters can change the sex of frogs and some fish, literally in midstream, at one point in their development, and there are the fish like *L. dimidiatus* that change their sex back and forth without the aid of science.

The sex of birds and mammals is more stable. Each species has its own patterns of mating behavior and in the lower orders the appropriate pattern is programmed into the brain of each individual, to be set in motion by hormones. The patterns dictate precisely what will be done, the hormone cycles dictate when. Outstanding recent research in this field by Frank Beach, M. W. Schein and E. B. Hale, T. R. Howell and G. A. Bartholomew, and Hilda Bruce has been covered more fully in Money and Ehrhardt (1972).

For subprimate species, partner selection seems to depend on proximity, not choice, but an experiment performed by Frank Beach raises questions about that. Some years ago, Beach tethered male dogs at points far apart in an open field and released bitches in heat to seek whichever male they wished as sex partners. Seven years later it happily occurred to Beach to repeat this part of the experiment, using the same dogs. The dogs had had no contact with each other during the long interval, but lo and behold, each female went straight to the same male the second time around, and after seven years!

Mating is initiated by a signal that may be visual, auditory, odiferous, or tactile, and when the initiatory signal evokes a suitable response, mating proceeds by means of reciprocal signals between male and female. With some species it's the male that gives the first signal. For birds, the signal may be a plumage display, courting dance, or mating call. Some birds, including jackdaws, greylag geese, and Adele penguins, stay with the same partners for life, but what brings a particular pair together in the first place is not known.

Experiments with turkeys and blackbirds have shown how visual signals rigidly control the sex life of these animals. Schein and Hale (1965) at Pennsylvania State University found that a tom turkey needs the visual signal of a hen turkey's head in order to position himself for copulation. Offered a choice between the head and the headless body of a stuffed, articulated hen turkey model, a frustrated experimental tom had to try to make it with the wire-mounted head.

Howell and Bartholomew found that a male Brewer blackbird can go through his mating pattern with a dummy female that has no wings as long as the dummy has either a head or a tail to serve as the signal. The blackbird could also respond to a dummy with a male-colored body if the dummy had a female head and neck. If the dummy had a female body but male head and neck, the bird was bewildered. He alighted on this female-bodied dummy and started to copulate, but when he got a closer look at the male head, he knocked the dummy down and pecked its head aggressively. A man who emerged similarly baffled from an encounter with a transvestite gave this human version of the blackbird's reaction:

"I was invited to this party. I have a few drinks and was sort of watching this cute girl, and eventually I start talking to her. We start rapping and carrying on. I mean she was really nice looking, you know, and my hopes built up real high. So I finally talk her into going out for a little drive with me, and we park the car on the side of the road. I was steady-talking and stuff, and she's throwing herself toward me, but she was kind of shy about letting people go up her leg. And it didn't feel exactly as soft or as slim as a girl should. So I started wondering and with a quick motion run my hand straight up her legs. And it sure wasn't a girl! I got mad with it and said a few bad words to her — or him — or whatever you want to call it — and told her to get her ass out, or him, just like that. Nobody likes to feel duped or fooled."

In mice, odors (pheromones) are major mating signals. In the experiments described earlier in this chapter, when Vandenbergh and his coworkers crowded adult female mice together without any males, they stopped ovulating, and when the odor of a male was then wafted to them, they all went into estrus together. Hilda Bruce found that if female mice were mated, the presence or even just the smell of a strange male interfered with the reproductive process; females exposed to the presence or odor of a strange male after they had copulated didn't get pregnant.

With most mammalian species, the female signals first, doing so by means of a vaginal odor. The same hormone cycle that starts ovulation releases the vaginal odor to let males know she is ready to become pregnant. Nearby

males respond automatically; their gallantry, programmed into their brains, is activated by the odor. Unless one of the males has already established his dominance, they will compete for the honor of serving her.

Up through the subprimates, mammals mate season-
ally, or only at times when the female is in estrus — that
is, at the ovulatory phase of her hormone cycle. (The mating behavior of cats and rabbits is even more tightly synchronized with ovulation, since copulation actually triggers the release of the female cat's or rabbit's egg so that
egg and sperm are brought together at the exact moment
of maximum fertility.) At all other times, subprimate
females do not emit the initiatory signal, and the males
are not aroused. Cyclic menstruation, which replaces
estrus in the old-world primate species, allows for more
latitude as to when a female can be sexually interested
and interesting, and the more sophisticated primate neocortex allows primates more latitude for experiments with
behavior that has not been programmed in. The fact that a
primate's brain is more immature, less finished, at birth
than the newborn subprimate's brain leaves the primate
brain more open to variety in what it learns.

The most primitive part of the brain, the core part that
developed more than two hundred million years ago, is
called the reptilian brain. The reptilian brain suffices for
the uncomplicated sex life of a lizard, snake or turtle, but
the mating behavior of subprimate mammals needs a
more modern layer, the limbic system or paleomammalian
brain. The limbic system can process enough information
to manage the sex life of mammals up through the rabbit.
The neocortex or neomammalian brain, the outside brain
layer, begins to appear in subprimate mammals, but subprimates could get along without a neocortex for their

sexual activities. Female primates could get by without it, too, but primate males and the more erotically versatile of their females need a neocortex to handle their more complicated sexual behavior. Without a neocortex,· humans could manage to procreate, but mating would lose its romance. There wouldn't be any Valentine's Day, any poetry or drama, and nobody would get excited by or about pornography. There might still be marriages, though, since even some birds' brains can prescribe life-long pair-bonding.

Nature chained sexual behavior to the sex hormone cycle to insure perpetuation of the species. Up to the primates, the chain is unbreakable, since it takes more neocortex than subprimates possess to break it. Subprimates can copulate only when the chances for reproduction are at their highest, and when that time comes, they have no choice; they must emit and obey a mating signal if they can. Some of the primates, however, have broken their hormonal bondage and achieved a small measure of autonomy in their sexual behavior. Male rhesus monkeys have been known to exercise choice to the extent of turning their backs on one mating partner for another more favored one when both the females were in heat. Female rhesus monkeys will mate for a few days after ovulation, and will play at mating with juvenile monkeys. Gorillas and chimpanzees copulate throughout the year, but they, like the rhesus monkeys, have an annual seasonal mating peak, and usually they mate at the ovulatory phase of the female's menstrual cycle.

The human species is the only one that has achieved complete freedom to engage in sexual behavior at any time of the month or year. There are still echoes of the evolutionary past, however, since most human females

175

show a peak of erotic interest associated with ovulation, though human females often also have a second peak associated with the menstrual period.

Freedom to copulate at times when the female partner is not fertile loosens the connection between sexual behavior and reproduction slightly among the other primates, but only humans can break the connection altogether. Only humans can plan conception, contraception, and sterilization so that a male and a female can take the bait of orgasm together without risking the hook of reproduction. Freedom to elaborate on the reproductive program laid down for the human species can enhance the bait considerably. Human beings derive luxurious sexual satisfaction from fantasy. They also can relish extragenital sex — those who stigmatize oral and anal sex as "bestial" simply don't know what they're talking about.

But freedom has its price. Freedom is freedom to make mistakes, and the more that can be learned, the greater the chance of learning it wrong. An adult rat, for example, whether it has ever had a chance to learn or not, can perform its full repertory of mating behavior, and must do so whenever opportunity and proper signal coincide. A monkey has more latitude than a rat in the behavior and timing of mating but a monkey that has had no chance to learn sexual behavior and practice it with other monkeys in childhood is hopeless at it as an adult.

Of all species, human beings have the broadest range of sexual behavior. They also have the most to learn, with the greatest chance of getting mixed up. The option of choosing one's time and partner brings anxiety about which time and partner to choose, and the option of rejecting a partner brings anxiety about being rejected. Thus humans can become fixated on unwilling sex partners, sex partners of the same sex, or inanimate objects. Only humans invent taboos that make some of them frigid or impotent; and only humans can be induced to renounce sex voluntarily.

Proximity and dominance still play a part in human pairing, but human beings complicate the business enormously with such uniquely human concerns as falling in love, property, and politics. These concerns distort mating patterns and work their way into tradition. As a melting pot, America is heir to a variety of dating and mating traditions, those of its original people and those imported with people from other parts of the world.

By far the most pervasive is the tradition of the virgin bride and double standard. This tradition probably originated in the Middle Eastern countries of the Mediterranean area long before biblical times, possibly when hamlets started growing into the cities that needed slaves to build and maintain them. At first the arrangement was polygamy, as described at a later date in the early books of the Old Testament. Allowing one male to monopolize several females is a form of erotic slavery. It has the practical societal advantage of making other males expendable, available to fight, and if need be, die, with less damage to the structure of the community. The expendable males don't get wives; for them there is only the public harem, the prostitutes. Such men could always hope to gain enough power to have wives of their own later. A public wife, however, could not hope to become a private wife later, although there have been a few outstanding exceptions to that rule.

Such a system is all of a piece with the concept of private property and patrilinear descent. It's quite easy to make sure who a child's mother is, but in societies where children inherit their names, position, and property from their fathers, the fathers yearn for cast-iron proof of paternity. The mothers yearn for it, too, since the patrilinear system puts their own and their children's security in jeopardy if the father doubts his paternity. It is noteworthy that those who have little private property and less pride of name to worry about — slaves and the poor — worry less about dating and mating traditions. By the same token, rebellion against the tyranny of private ownership in our society today is often coupled with rebellion against monogamy.

Although proof of paternity is practically impossible to provide even with the scientific methods available today, the search for it has often gone to extraordinary lengths, including the insistence on virginity in brides, virtual or literal enslavement of women, their physical or cultural imprisonment, and brainwashing them to deny their own sexuality.

As polygamy gave way to an official policy of monogamous marriage, the men who could afford it clung to their sexual freedom through dalliance and adultery, maintaining mistresses instead of harems. Some of the higher-ranking men invented a duty to improve the peasant or slave stock by favoring the more delectable daughters of the lower classes with their seed. As long as more people were needed, society protested only perfunctorily. Until fairly recently, the real penalty for being a bastard in Christian cultures was not to be disgraced but to get no inheritance.

Although modified by conditions in the New World, time, and various liberation movements, the early Mediterranean tradition is still the official formula for American dating and mating. Other American traditions are in sharp contrast. In American Samoa, for example, the great Polynesian kinship family tradition survives. There it would be socially and politically presumptuous for a man to set himself up as head of a family in a monogamous marriage before he was thirty years old. He awaits the dignity of age. In adolescence and young adulthood, both sexes are free to conduct love affairs as their fancy takes them. It is traditional for a virgin to take as his or her first partner a slightly older girl or boy who has had some sexual experience. Offspring are welcomed into the great kinship household of their mother or their father, as they in turn will welcome their grandchildren and other kin under the extended-family roof which they will establish eventually. When he turns thirty, a man becomes monogamous, marries, establishes himself as the head of a household and economic unit, and takes his place as a participant in the system of government.

There is also in America the slave tradition of obligatory breeding without the right to marry, which was superimposed on the sometimes matriarchal extended-family traditions of the Africans who were brought to the New World as slaves. The permanence of any slave-breeding partnership was solely at the discretion of the owner. While the young parents and older children did the heavy work in the field, the old and infirm stayed in the yard to care for the small children. As soon as a girl was old enough, she was required to start breeding to increase the assets of the owner. Only partially modified, this tradition lives on in rural areas and urban ghettos, where the system of subsistence welfare payments has replaced the plantation system of subsistence payment in kind. One result is to perpetuate short-term liaisons and breeding partnerships. The young mothers still go out to do underpaid work, as do the fathers if they can find jobs, and the care of the children still devolves on the grandparents. A man usually settles down with a wife rather late in life and becomes stepgrandfather to her young grandchildren. Although this system is much criticized by taxpayers and moralists, there is nothing intrinsically wrong with it except the lack of solid economic underpinnings for the families and the refusal of the larger society which follows the Mediterranean tradition to acknowledge its validity.

There is also in America today the tradition of betrothal and sexual equality, a rural tradition with very ancient roots in the Scandinavian culture, the culture of the North. Historically, this tradition has been traced through eastern Europe and south as far as the Alps. Transplanted to colonial New England, it appeared there in the form of bundling, but in Scandinavia it was known as night courting. The girls on a farm were given separate sleeping quarters away from the main farmhouse during the summer. A band of boys would sally forth of an evening to serenade the girls in their "night feet houses" and when a boy and a girl felt drawn to each other, their friends would leave them to spend the night alone together. For the first few nights, he was expected to remain fully clothed and stay on top of the bedcovers, but if the romance progressed she would invite him under the covers. Even then he would keep his clothes on. Only when they felt sure of their feelings would he undress and they would then make love. After that they would announce their betrothal. Betrothal was as solemn and binding as a marriage ceremony, and culminated in marriage when the bride got pregnant. If the couple failed to achieve a pregnancy, there was no wedding and the betrothal lapsed. This tradition has left traces on modern Scandinavia, where young people today enjoy far more freedom to love and live together before marriage than do those in the Roman Catholic countries to the south.

The modern version of the betrothal tradition, so admirably suited to the age of contraception and early puberty, has diffused to America as the older Scandinavian tradition did before it. It is being adopted enthusiastically by groups of young people across the country, whether or not they know anything about its venerable origins. At a recent seminar on sex in childhood, Povl Toussieng (1971), a psychiatrist and pediatrician at the University of Oklahoma medical school, described the clash between traditions this way.

It looks like no commitment when two young people are living together and they're not married. They're spending practically all their waking and sleeping hours together, and they're sharing a great deal. It's beautiful to watch, but to their parents, it's living in sin. The parents continue to press, "Why don't you get him to make a commitment to you?" Now how can you make more of a commitment than spending twenty-four hours a day with each other? So, therefore, I really think that the word commitment will be redefined, just like responsibility will be redefined. They will have new meanings, but they will still be there.

All cultures prescribe limitations on the choice of sex partners, and so, by implication, on the choice of people one is permitted to fall in love with. The star-crossed lovers of legend — Romeo and Juliet, Petrarch and Laura, Launcelot and Guinevere, and the others — are those who defied such cultural limitations. Taboo lines may be drawn by caste, class, tribe, religion, totem, politics, or financial status, but almost without exception known cultures, primitive as well as civilized, have a powerful taboo against sexual transgression of close blood kinship — the incest taboo.

Various explanations of why incest is so all but universally proscribed have been offered, but none of them is completely satisfactory. The incest taboo has been attributed to the widespread belief that incestuous breeding produces physical and mental degeneration through exaggeration of bad hereditary characteristics but not of good ones, which any good stock breeder knows is a fallacy. Two examples often cited in support of this belief are the imperial Hapsburg family of Europe and the Jackson Whites, a long-isolated community in the Ramapo Mountains on the border between New York and New Jersey. Neither example proves very much.

In their efforts to hold their empire together, the Hapsburgs didn't hesitate to marry their uncles, aunts and first cousins. By the time Leopold I succeeded to the scepter in 1657, it's true that the underslung Hapsburg jaw was so exaggerated in him that he couldn't close his mouth. Not even the flattery of the court painters could disguise the fact that he looked like a simpleton, but that didn't keep him from being an effective and popular sovereign for almost half a century.

The Jackson Whites had wildly heterogeneous origins. Jackson was an eighteenth-century Britisher who did his bit during the Revolutionary War by kidnaping English girls to serve as prostitutes for the British troops in America. Hounded out of New York when the war ended, these women took to the hills along with some Hessian deserters and Tuscarora Indians and stayed there in seclusion. Continuous interbreeding in this exotic community was interrupted briefly when some runaway slaves found haven there during the Civil War period, but eventually isolation, intermarriage, poor education, and inadequate diet combined to produce a fairly homogeneous, culturally impoverished community. Genealogically discovered during World War II, the Jackson Whites have been studied by social scientists seeking ammunition in the nature-nurture battle, each side interpreting the findings as support.

As a foundation for the incest taboo, the biological degeneracy theory does not hold up. While plants and animals are, of course, routinely inbred to exaggerate some of their characteristics, success depends on ruthless pruning in each generation. To achieve degeneration, incestuous parents would have to eliminate their normal offspring for several generations. Surveying the literature on father-daughter incest among the Incas, Egyptians, and royal families of Hawaii, Franco Ferracuti (1972) of the University of Puerto Rico could find no direct relationship between intrafamilial breeding and degeneracy.

"Degenerate traits have not been reported in the progeny of those who had no incest taboo," Ferracuti concluded.

Cleopatra, the last of the Ptolemies, was the product of twelve generations of incest, and it would be difficult to consider her an example of somatic degeneration. In the United States, a study of the people resident in the mountains of Kentucky, among whom exogamous fertilization is rare, shows areas in which epilepsy and mental disorder have high incidences and others in which the younger generation is perfectly healthy and in fact physically superior to the average.

183

An exploded but still popular assumption is that incest avoidance is an instinctive protection for children from their parents' sexuality during the Oedipal phase when a boy rehearses adult behavior by vying with his father for his mother's love, a girl with her mother for her father's. However, explanations of incest avoidance as instinctive have been completely rejected by scientific investigators.

A report from Israel sheds a completely different light on the incest taboo. Joseph Shepher (Money and Ehrhardt, 1972) of Haifa studied the first 2,769 marriages of Israelis who were born in the kibbutzim of Israel's three major kibbutz federations. Kibbutz children live in the close proximity of their own special infants' dwelling. They play together constantly and, since sex play is not frowned upon either overtly or covertly, practically all of them engage in sexual play with each other. As the ones who are reared there grow up together as children and adolescents, it could be expected that they would eventually find marital partners among the members of their own group. They are not blood kin, and there is nothing in the community attitudes or tradition that would discourage such partnerships.

Yet of the nearly three thousand marriages that the kibbutz-born children had contracted up to the time of Shepher's study, not one couple was made up of two people who had lived together in the same infants' dwelling uninterruptedly during their first five years of life! Furthermore, there weren't even any known love affairs between two such people. The amorous relations of the inhabitants of one kibbutz in particular were well documented by the investigator. It was not that the individuals themselves had tried to suppress such relationships or that the elders tried to prevent them. They just simply didn't happen.

The young people themselves seem to take the impossibility for granted. Shepher gives this description of a reunion between two twenty-two-year-olds who had grown up in the same kibbutz. She is lovely, dressed for a festive evening out. He has just returned from the wars on leave, tall and handsome in his uniform. They greet each other with obvious delight. "What a pity we're classmates," he says. "We'd make a beautiful couple!" Both laugh heartily, and they go on their way.

Perhaps the incest taboo is not a cultural or moral veto but a negative function of the ability to fall in love, a negative imprinting that prevents you from falling in love with anyone you knew intimately throughout those first years of your life, whether or not they are members of your family.

7.   The Sex Revolution

THE ABILITY TO SEPARATE THE BAIT of sexual pleasure from the hook of reproduction sparked a revolution more momentous for the human race than any in history. After smoldering through the ages, it began to spread in this century, and none too soon. It took the human race several hundred thousand years to build a population of one billion by 1850, but only a century after that there were almost three billion people living in the world, and by 1980 there will probably be four billion. Of all the pollution problems that must be solved, people pollution is among the most threatening. Once a luxury, the separation of recreational sex from procreational sex is today an urgent necessity.

The revolution started when primates began to copulate

at times when the female was not fertile. The human species took the next step, discovering how to get off the reproduction hook by inducing abortion. There's no knowing when this step was taken since it happened long before writing was invented. Primitive contraception probably dates back almost as far as induced abortion, for a four-thousand-year-old Egyptian relic, the Petri Papyrus, describes a number of ways of averting pregnancy. Both abortion and contraception were improvements on infanticide, which has also been widely practiced in human societies.

After these beginnings, the revolution smoldered along for ages with little to fuel it. Whatever the feelings of the individuals in each instance, societal wisdom lay in maximizing human fertility. With too few people in the world, life expectancy short, infant mortality high, and plagues killing off thousands at irregular intervals, a couple had to start breeding pretty quickly after puberty and keep at it if they hoped to see their surviving progeny through childhood before they themselves were dead.

The preposterous theory that women are incapable of enjoying sex — a theory that has robbed untold numbers of both men and women of so much of their sexual birthright — fitted in with society's need for women to concentrate their time and energy on gestation and lactation. Impregnation being less of a drain on the time and energy of fathers, society could afford to allow men more latitude for recreational sex as long as their wives and children were provided for and protected, Hence the double standard.

Marriage is so ancient that no one can say when or where it began, but obviously it was designed primarily for procreation and child nurture. Marriage encourages sexual intercourse, provides for the protection and rearing of children, and recognizes the fact that children need the guidance of adults of both sexes.

The Judeo-Christian religion made marriage a sacred rite, as had older religions, and then went further by making sex of any kind outside the bonds of marriage a sin. The early Christian fathers outdid themselves by making the enjoyment of sex a sin even within the marriage relationship, lest it detract from the solemnity of the duty to procreate. The final step was to proscribe feelings of sexual pleasure within the privacy of dreams and fantasy, which forced the faithful to load themselves with guilt for the dreams that escaped their control. The Inquisition hounded such sinners unmercifully, and was willing to burn them at the stake, especially if they were women. Sex dreams that wore even the flimsiest disguise could, however, be mistaken for evidence of saintliness if they were masochistic enough.

The ban against enjoyment of conjugal sex has largely crumbled. Its inhibiting effects are still felt, but our culture now widely accepts the idea that both marriage partners ought to enjoy their sexual relations, even when they are not bent on increasing the population. (Ironically, the "ought to" seems to inhibit some people and cause them as much anxiety as the "shalt not" did others.) The main controversies over recreational sex now rage on the premarital and extramarital fronts.

Those who stirred the sex revolution into flame were an incongruous lot. Margaret Sanger and other prophets of birth control might still be crying in the wilderness but for the help of some people who would be astounded to hear themselves hailed as sex revolutionaries. Our candidates are Charles Goodyear who, in 1839, happened on a way of vulcanizing rubber, and his English contemporary, Alexander Parkes, who seven years later devised cold vulcanizing, a process that makes thin-walled rubber items tough and pliant. Then there was Robert Ingersoll, whose "dollar watch" fortune proved that mass distribution of an item at a low price can be more profitable than catering to the carriage trade, and Henry Ford, godfather of the assembly line. When the bonfires they started met, one of the many disruptive results was to flood the country during the 1920s with the rubber condom, the world's first reliable, inexpensive, readily available, and uninhibitory contraceptive. Though one of the birthday gifts to the country unveiled at the Philadelphia Exposition of 1876, on the occasion of the nation's first centennial, had been a rubber condom, it wasn't until the 1920s that the latex process made condoms so tissue-thin as to be widely acceptable, as well as cheap and effective. By the end of the decade, a condom could be bought anonymously from a vending machine in the men's room of almost any gas station in the country or from a drugstore for a quarter or less.

Pessaries and diaphragms also became popular, giving women their own pregnancy veto, but they were more expensive and more trouble because they were supposed to be fitted by a doctor. Condoms have the further advantage of offering some protection against the spread of venereal disease. Although few men had that in mind when buying them, condoms could legally be offered for sale as hygienic devices in states with laws prohibiting the sale of contraceptives.

While vulcanization, mass production, and mass distribution scattered sex-revolutionary sparks across the land, the Great Depression spread the flame like wildfire. A dip in the national birth rate between 1930 and 1940 shows that some ten million U.S. babies who could have been expected never arrived. Ten million is several times the total number of U.S. military deaths in all the wars this country has ever fought — happy evidence that contraception is a far more efficient, as well as beneficent, means of controlling population growth than war.

Spectacular progress in death control underscored the need for birth control by boosting the population at the other end of the life span. Death control stretched an American child's life expectancy at birth from forty-seven years in 1900 to seventy-one years in 1970. Death control also radically revised the pattern of American life. While former generations expected to spend their adult lives procreating and providing for their children, the gift of those extra years from medical science and public health measures, plus earlier puberty and smaller families, mean that Americans today have perhaps half their lives still ahead of them when their youngest child leaves home. That "second lifetime" after procreational responsibilities have been fulfilled offers golden opportunities for recreational sex, but puts enormous strain on our cultural stereotypes of human pairing, which were designed for shorter lives. Choosing a partner for a procreative quarter of a century is not the same thing as choosing a partner for a half-century that includes an extended adolescence on one side and an extended middle and old age on the other side of a reproductive period.

Allen Wheelis (1958) provides an apt metaphor in *The Quest for Identity,* although he was not writing specifically of marriage.

This is of relevance in comparing the unsure man of today with his very sure grandfather. . . . The identity of his grandfather was like the log cabin of the frontier . . . small and dark, but it was put up with dispatch and was sturdy and snug. The grandson is fumbling as a builder . . . but it is to be noted that his job is harder. The materials with which he must work are more variegated. Their proper integration would achieve not a log cabin, but a more complicated and interesting structure, admitting more light and air and providing more room for living.

Most Americans participate in the sex revolution to the extent of practicing contraception but neglect to look beyond birth and death statistics to the wider horizons that the revolution opens up. They see the sex explorations of youth as the normal restlessness of adolescence aggravated by permissive upbringing and the adult pioneers as assorted freaks and malcontents seeking gratification of perverted tastes. It can no longer escape their notice that overpopulation and technological advances are creating formidable problems and that the world is getting overcrowded with people, but they do not see that if our culture is to survive, our sexual life-styles will have to adapt to these changes. Once that imperative is generally recognized, there will be more tolerance of those who are exploring various possible alternatives to the presently accepted sexual norms.

Among the pioneers of change, several groups are called liberationists, although their goals are by no means the same. There are women seeking liberation from educational, economic, political, and social discrimination; men seeking liberation from unrelenting competitive pressures and emotional repression; and homosexuals and transvestites seeking liberation from opprobrium and penalties for adopting the only kinds of sexual life-styles that have meaning for them. Then there are the young people seeking forms of pairing suitable for their extended adolescence; married couples seeking wider sexual freedom within the institution of marriage; single adults seeking a legitimate sex life outside of marriage; and old people protesting the assumption that their sex lives are over. The only common goal of all these groups is to make the cultural stereotypes allow for their needs. Only the transexuals, desperately absorbed in their own search for unity of gender identity and role, cling to the conventional stereotypes; they seek only the right to exchange one stereotype for the other. There is also a group of practicing bisexuals who might be called expansionists.

The encounter groups that so quickly took root on both coasts and spread across the country in wide variety seek to open the approaches to all the pioneer camps by clearing away the underbrush of conventional forms that screen individuals from each other.

The conventional body of our society is bounded on one side by securely heterosexual, happily mated adults, who don't feel constricted by the stereotypes or threatened by change and who may never have heard of an encounter group, and on the other side by those who cling desperately to every conventional sex role distinction, no matter how trivial, lest any relaxation in the stereotype destroy their shaky confidence in themselves as male or female. If you find yourself somewhere in between these two extremes, there are two things for you to keep in mind.

First, we are all pioneers. Eagerly or reluctantly, we are moving forward into unknown territory, driven by inexorable forces. The fact that we, not nature, are responsible for those forces — overpopulation, longevity, technology, and contraception — doesn't soften nature's ultimatum that we must adapt to the changes they bring or perish. Adaptation depends on maintaining a workable balance between stability and flexibility. A society that relies on narrow, rigid stereotypes must break out of them or stagnate. But a group of people whose cultural stereotypes are too loose or too fragmented to support cooperation is not a society at all, it's a collection of people whose only hope of survival lies in quickly tightening up their stereotypes (one reason a successful revolution so often ends in the welcome of a tyrant). The healthy society is one that tolerates experimentation with a variety of adaptive responses within its stereotypes. In times of rapid change, it takes such a society to survive the strains. Thanks to overpopulation and contraception, we can afford tolerance of experimentation with alternatives to the familiar life-styles geared to procreation.

Our society no longer tries to restrict its members to one form of religion, as some societies still do. Where an established church once felt compelled to torture and kill those who wouldn't or couldn't conform, we now tolerate a wide variety of religious denominations. We respect the right of individuals to express their spirituality in the form that makes them most comfortable with themselves and their consciences, or in no form at all, demanding only that each respect the rights of others. The sexual rebellions, schisms, and splinter groups of today reflect the need for similar tolerance of variety in the ways a man is allowed to be a man, a woman to be a woman.

The second thing to keep in mind is that you don't have to join any of the pioneer camps, or even approve of them, in order to benefit from their explorations. If you believe that all the trails now being explored are leading the pioneers to disaster, remember that in unknown territory, a map of trails that end in morasses and cul de sacs can be very useful indeed.

Liberationists — Women

The women's liberation movement is the largest of the pioneer groups. It includes a confusing variety of subgroups, each with a set of specific goals and programs for attaining them. Basic to all the women's subgroups is protest against the underlying fact that the conventional stereotype of a woman is of an inferior human being. Losing is built into our culture's script for women, so one cannot meet the standards set for women and also the standards set for adults. There is ample evidence of this classic no-win option for women, but a single experiment is enough to illustrate the point.

Inge K. Broverman and her coworkers (1970) at Worcester (Mass.) State Hospital gave their subjects a test designed to elicit the psychological profile of a person they would consider healthy, mature, and socially competent. The subjects, all of them clinically trained psychologists, psychiatrists or social workers, were people one could expect to be more intellectually independent of social conventions than the average person. They were divided into three groups, each group including both men and women. One group was asked to pick from a long list the traits that would characterize a healthy, mature, socially competent person; the second group was asked to pick from the same list the traits that would characterize such a man; and the third group, those that would characterize such a woman.

The three profiles that emerged showed that the group's concept of an ideal person was almost identical with the concept of an ideal man but not very much like the concept of an ideal woman. In other words, the better the woman you are in our society, the less of a person you are, even in the eyes of people with the training and experience in working with people as individuals these subjects had.

What helps to distort the female stereotype is that our culture equates femininity with passive dependence, using as a springboard the fact that sperm seek ova, and that a man's penis must be active to impregnate a woman, whereas a woman's ovum can be impregnated even if her clitoris and vagina are totally anesthetized. In fact, although sperm and ovum meet inside the woman's body, the ovum comes to meet the sperm through the fallopian tubes just as the sperm comes to meet the ovum through the vas deferens and urethra. And, as noted in Chapter 5, it is just as logical to say that the egg fertilizes the sperm as that the sperm fertilizes the egg. Men and women who accept passive dependence but not activity as feminine don't know what they're missing, and they lose out in other ways as well as in sexual recreation.

A passive, dependent woman can be impregnated all right, even an unconscious woman can be, but judged solely as a procreator, a passive, dependent woman is not very good at her job. Julia Sherman (1972), a psychologist at the University of Wisconsin, reported to the American Association for the Advancement of Science that "one of the most common types among women who have spontaneously aborted their babies three or more times for no known physical reason is the excessively dependent woman." She mentioned the dismay of Harvey Peskin, a psychologist at San Francisco State College, at discovering that the more "masculine" women among his subjects for research on menstruation had been independently rated as more maternal, more attractive, and more competent in their sex roles than the more "feminine" subjects. "Female sexual-caste prescriptions," Sherman concluded, "encourage women to become inferior, incompetent human beings which in turn is used to justify their inferior status."

Our society puts plenty of pressure on girls and women to conform to the standard of the feminine stereotype, but offers them few rewards for excellence, even in the areas marked out for women. The economic rewards for doing the work of a wife, homemaker, and mother are no greater if the work is done expertly than if it is skimped or hardly done at all, and while an expert secretary may be many times more valuable to a business operation than a poor one, there is seldom very much difference in their pay. There are, however, some rewards for feminine *in*competence, as a recent Parker Pen advertisement illustrated blatantly. "You might as well give her a gorgeous pen to keep her checkbook *un*balanced with," the copy read. "A sleek and shining pen will make her feel prettier. Which is more important to any girl than solving mathematical mysteries." To really appreciate what this kind of stereotype does to gender pride, try recasting the ad in masculine terms. With a cultural definition of femininity that can make such an ad possible, it's hardly surprising that the prospect of professional success can inspire in a woman the kind of anxiety that the prospect of professional failure inspires in men, as a number of experiments by Matina Horner, now president of Radcliffe College, and others have demonstrated.

Pay discrimination is another formidable handicap to women's pride of gender. In our market-oriented society, pay is notoriously low in the fields that rely mainly on women employees — child care, grammar school teaching, clerical office work, and domestic labor — and in employment generally, the women who work alongside men were being paid an average of 40 percent less than men doing the same work in 1970. Male-to-female transexuals commonly have this sex differential brought vividly home to them by the drop in their income when they become female instead of male employees in the same line of work. Unless they make a new career for themselves as high-priced entertainers or call girls, they often find it hard to pay for their sex-change operations. By contrast, female-to-male transexuals, whose more complicated operations cost four or more times as much, find the financial strain eased. When they get jobs as men, their paychecks commonly are higher even if the new job is in the same field at the same level as before.

Women get shortchanged on recognition as well as on pay, even when their work is judged by other women, as an experiment by Philip Goldberg (1968), a psychologist at Connecticut College, demonstrated. College women were asked to evaluate a series of professional articles. The sets of articles that went to each evaluator were identical except for the first names of the authors, so that a particular article which might have the by-line of John Smith, for example, in one set of papers showed Joan Smith as the author in another set, and so on. For a

number of the papers, the same paper got a higher rank-
ing from the evaluators who thought the author was a
man than from those who thought the author was a
woman, although all the evaluations were done by
women.

In short, the stereotype says that the ideal woman is not
a very good human being. If a woman is feminine she's
incompetent, if she's competent she's not feminine, and
the value of whatever she does except procreate will be
downgraded because it was done by a woman. Protesting
such systematic erosion of their pride of gender is anything but a rejection of female gender identity/role, yet
that is how a great many men and some women view the
women's liberation movement. Men still give, and women
still accept, as a compliment the comment "She thinks
like a man." Women who fall into the trap of trying to
think and act like men give themselves an impossible
handicap, since almost any man has a practically un-
beatable head start on them at thinking and acting like a
man. The liberating goal is to make it possible for a
woman to achieve pride, confidence, and competence
without having to reject her femininity.

Why do so many women still champion the stereotypes
that discriminate against them? In January 1903 George
Bernard Shaw gave part of the answer when he wrote to
Clement Wood.

A slave state is always ruled by those who can get around the
masters; that is, by the more cunning of the slaves themselves.
No fascinating woman ever wants to be emancipated . . . her
object is to gather power into the hands of Man because she
knows she can govern him. . . . It is only the proud, straightforward women who wish, not to govern, but to be free, that
object to slavery.

Liberationists — Men

It's harder to perceive the masculine stereotype of our society as a handicap because it fits our stereotype of a human being, yet it is almost equally stultifying. A woman may find her vocational options limited, her intellectual development stunted, and her physical activities curtailed. It's a man's emotional development that is stunted by the stereotype, and while his physical and intellectual horizons are wide, the goals are set by competition, so that no matter what he does, it is never enough. The masculine stereotype requires a man to achieve and dominate in never-ending competition. If he makes a million dollars the multimillionaires still taunt him. No matter how much of the world he may dominate he cannot be content with it, as Alexander the Great, Napoleon, Hitler, and others have so disastrously demonstrated. "Rat race" and "treadmill" are words men use to describe their lot, and with good reason.

As the price of intensive procreation men were saddled with the main burden of the family breadwinning. Although this burden has been eased considerably now that wives are gainfully employed in some 40 percent of all U.S. husband-wife households, the stereotype still ties a man's worth to his work, whether it's the family's only economic lifeline or not. He is not allowed to build his gender pride and confidence on what he is, only on what he does, and since past performance is heavily discounted, he must keep doing until he drops. This concept can make a man's retirement years few and miserable, instead of the "harvest years" they're supposed to be, and doom his wife to years of widowhood.

A man is also expected to perform indefatigably as a cocksman, leaving no attractive woman unturned, so to speak, and no matter how successful he may be, the all-pervasive spirit of competition is there to spoil his pleasure by whispering that perhaps there are other men who do better. Nor can he enjoy a purely friendly relationship with a woman since he, she, or society, and probably all three, will distort the relationship by assuming it is a sexual one. Besides destroying his potential for friendship with half the human race, the stereotype taints a man's friendships with other men with the fear of homosexuality. Although our society has begun to ease its harsh treatment of avowed homosexuals a little, that fear still makes men excessively wary of their friendly reactions to other men and sets narrow limits on the way they permit themselves to show whatever love the competitive spirit allows them to feel for other men.

Competition also robs men's sport of its highest value. Play for the pure joy of the game is contaminated with the purpose of winning. Stereotypic men quickly lose interest in the games they can't win, and prefer to learn new games by paying a pro to dragoon them past the "shameful" stage of ineptness. Sandlot baseball for all the kids on the block gives way to Little League, which selects out the boys who can win games against other selected teams.

Our male stereotype also dictates that a man be a good father, but gives him no training and little time for it. A normal interest in dolls and babies is firmly discouraged in boyhood, and only at the tag end of the day and on weekends and vacations do most men have the chance to be practicing fathers. A woman can ask for a job that enables her to spend part of the day with her children, and possibly even find one; a man would risk being laughed out of the personnel office. A man who applies for paternity leave so that he can take his full part in what may be the most meaningful period of his family life still makes the headlines. A navy captain who turned down a sailor's request personified the stereotype when he said, "Dammit no. I can see why you had to be there for the laying of the keel, but not why you have to be there for the launching." Through the ages women have done much to foster this attitude by denying fathers any role in the drama of childbirth, and for generations doctors, more concerned about delivery room efficiency and possible infection than about what makes a family, relegated fathers to the waiting room.

American men are not required, as in some cultures, to cultivate scars on their faces to show how tough they are, but the stereotypic demand for toughness scars and cripples them in other ways almost from birth. A man must be able to take it, whatever "it" may be, without whimpering. "Men don't cry" is one of the first and greatest commandments of the American masculine mystique. It's hard to see any functional value in this commandment, and the cost is high. As an example, Warren Farrell (1974) gives this description of a highway accident. The steering mechanism of a couple's car had failed while she was driving, and they had collided with a bus.

The people in the bus piled out to help them. The women went up to Joyce, took her aside, asked if she was upset, and created the conditions which encouraged her to obtain needed relief by crying. The men approached Larry, who was also totally shaken, and said, "Wow, that was a close one, man — are you sure you're OK? How's the car?" For the next five minutes they discussed problems with steering mechanisms and other mechanical difficulties. When Larry and Joyce returned to the car they were both aware of the tremendous tension Larry still had pent up within him, as well as the relief from the tension Joyce felt [although she was the one who had been driving when the accident occurred]. By allowing Joyce to appear weak, society allowed her to gain internal strength, while Larry suffered the consequences of surface strength.

If a man does express himself by crying, it can cost him even more dearly, as Senator Edmund Muskie discovered. Muskie's 1972 campaign to win his party's presidential nomination hit the skids after he let himself be goaded to tears by attacks on his wife. The price of crying is exacted on everyday levels, too. Farrell tells of a friend who once, when personal tragedies and frustrations had mounted overwhelmingly, broke down and cried in front of an office colleague.

"The news of my crying was all over the office in an hour," the man remembers vividly. "At first nobody said anything, they just sort of looked. One of the guys did joke, 'Hear you and Sally been crying lately, eh?' I guess that was a jibe at my masculinity, but the knowing silence of the others indicated the same doubts. What really hurt was that two years later, when I was doing very well and being considered for a promotion, it was brought up again. While my manager was looking over my evaluation, he read a paragraph to himself and said, 'What do you think about that crying incident?' You can bet that was the last time I let myself cry."

After stunting and deforming a man's emotional development, the "tough" stereotype bars him from seeking professional medical help for emotional disorders. Men are no more immune to depression, for example, than to stomach ulcers, but men who wouldn't hesitate to consult a doctor for a persistent bellyache wouldn't dare to consult a psychiatrist for a persistent depression-ache, and those who have the good sense to do so are constrained to keep it a dark secret. Senator Muskie may have lost a Democratic primary, but Senator Eagleton was unceremoniously booted out of the 1972 vice-presidential race as soon as it became known that he had taken treatment for depression some years before.

Why men cling to the stereotype that costs them so dearly in these and other ways is fairly obvious. A system that force-feeds a man's ego with the assurance that he is per se more intelligent, more stable, and more valuable than half of his peers, and on top of that gets him out of a lot of household drudgery, is hard to reject. Nevertheless, even the male natives are growing restless and a men's liberation movement is taking shape. In 1974 there were some four hundred men's consciousness-raising groups meeting regularly in the United States to share the conviction that the satisfaction of being a lord and master is a poor substitute for a real partner in sex, love, procreation, and work, and to encourage each other in the exercise of those aspects of their emotional natures that were stunted by the masculine stereotype.

A favorite theme of the antiliberationists is that the movement seeks to blur the differences between the sexes. Nothing of the sort. The women's liberationists are not saying they want to be men; they are saying, "Don't make us forgo femininity as the price of our development as individuals, including intellectual and physical development and a chance to compete for the rewards of achievement in our market-oriented society." Men's liberationists are not saying they want to be women, they are saying, "Don't make denial of our masculinity the price of our

203

development as individuals, including the emotional and nurturant side of our nature." Neither claims that all men should be emotional and nurturant or that all women should be giant brains and athletes. The claim is that both society and the individual will benefit if those who have these potentials are free to develop them according to their capability and taste without having their masculinity or femininity impugned. Since the conditions that once made it necessary for men to suppress their capacity for emotion and nurturance whatever it might be, and to deny women their full intellectual and physical development whatever it might be, no longer prevail, the claim is eminently reasonable.

Gender stereotypes are built on the genital and reproductive function differences between the sexes and filled in by the sex differences that derive from them. They are finished and trimmed with culturally assigned differences in sexual behavior, work, and play that facilitate cooperation. The liberationists are saying that the structures will better serve their purposes today, and will make life richer, if some of the trim is transferred to the human schema and if the Victorian gingerbread is discarded altogether. Far from blurring sex differences, to do so would focus attention on the basic structures.

There is promise of rich reward for men and women liberationists in the scattered evidences that boys who are not afraid of the "feminine" side of their nature and girls who have been allowed to pursue their "masculine" as well as their "feminine" interests are often above average in general intelligence and creativity. Furthermore, a number of observers have noted a special warmth and ease in the relations between parents and children after the father has participated in the birth of the children.

Such good early fathering continues to pay dividends, according to a survey made by two psychologists, Mark Reuter and Henry Biller, as reported in the January 1974 issue of *Human Behavior*. Of 172 male undergraduates they tested, Reuter and Biller found that the young men who turned out the most well-adjusted had very loving fathers who were around a good deal of the time, while the sons of unloving fathers who were also around a lot tested out as undependable and immature. If such findings as these are consolidated and confirmed, the bonus for pioneering is obviously worthwhile indeed.

Liberationists — Others

Gay liberationists, transvestites, and transexuals are not trying to blur sex differences any more than are the men and women liberationists. Homosexuals resent being penalized because in them parts of one gender schema have been incorporated into the other gender schema. Transvestites similarly resent being penalized because they can switch the coding of their schemas and have a compulsion to do so. Transexuals want to alter their own genital structures to achieve unity of gender identity/role. Some members of these groups may consider themselves superior to ordinary mortals, but, unlike the women's and men's liberationists, none advocates altering the gender stereotypes, not even the trim. In fact, they are far more likely to exaggerate the trim than condemn it. Members of these groups are typically among the most ardent champions of the conventional sex stereotypes.

An effeminate homosexual man is likely to caricature,

and a male transvestite in his female role to personify, the conventional stereotype of a woman rather than any actual woman. Most transexuals embrace the stereotype of their identity-sex enthusiastically and uncritically, even a person as sophisticated as Jan Morris. In reviewing Morris's autobiography for the *New York Times Book Review* (April 14, 1974), Rebecca West noted that the author "sounds not like a woman, but like a man's idea of a woman, and curiously enough, the idea of a man not nearly so intelligent as James Morris used to be . . . like a woman in a TV commercial."

A group that many people find especially frightening is the bisexuals. These are people who see no reason to confine their erotic interest to the members of only one sex. They seek freedom to expand their expressions of friendship with members of both sexes to include close body contact and sexual relations. They may alternate between a sex partner who is male and one who is female (episodic homosexuality) or engage in sex play with a man and a woman or with a larger mixed group at the same time. It would be more accurate to call them ambisexuals.

The size of this group and its growth potential are impossible to estimate. While it's true, as noted in Chapter 1, that we all start out ambisexual, our culture has so rigidly proscribed ambisexuality for so long that the gate of erotic interest has undoubtedly locked tight in one direction or the other for some proportion of the adults in our society. There is ample reason to believe, however, that this gate would stay open if encouraged by the cultural stereotypes, as it did in ancient Greece. Furthermore, there is evidence that the gate can close without locking so that the direction of erotic interest can be reversed, as is done in cultures like that of the Batak people of Lake Toba, also mentioned in Chapter 1. The people of these cultures are ambisexual in stages — homosexual in adolescence, heterosexual as adults — as prescribed by their traditions.

In our own society, women have much more freedom than men to express their feelings of friendship and affection for members of their own sex in close body contact (but not sexual relations). While there is not yet enough evidence to support a conclusion, what evidence has been gathered indicates that among the swingers who have been initiated into homosexual contacts, the women find it easier to accept such contacts than the men.

There is plenty of evidence that bisexual group sex can be as personally satisfying as a paired partnership provided each participant is "tuned in" on the same wave length. This might not be easy to achieve, since known bisexuals are nearly always more attracted to partners of one sex than of the other. The ratio of attraction to men and women may be 60:40, say, or 25:75, but only in a very few instances is it 50:50. And the possibility that an ambisexual will fall equally in love with two people, a man and a woman, in a threesome relationship, seems to be extremely remote.

Before anyone could say whether or not all humans are capable of developing a bisexual gender identity/role and giving it bisexual erotic expression, an entire generation would have to grow up in a society that openly sanctioned, practiced, and taught by example bisexual love. That would be a good thing or a bad thing, depending on how you feel about the fellowship of humankind, but it's hardly likely to happen here in the next few generations.

While all these groups are called liberationists, they do not operate in the same areas, as the following table shows.

TRANSPOSITIONS AFFECTING GENDER IDENTITY

	MAJOR	INTERMEDIATE	MINOR
Enduring	Transexualism	Obligative homosexualism	Type of career
Episodic	Transvestism	Bisexualism	Type of recreation

The transposition made by transexuals and transvestites involves the complete redirection of their own gender identities; the transposition made by homosexuals and bisexuals involves mainly the part of their gender identity tied into the direction of their erotic interest. The transpositions advocated by men and women liberationists do not involve erotic gender identity; they are in the peripheral areas of work and play. In fact what they seek is not so much transposition as decoding the activities that society has defined as appropriate for one sex but not for the other for societal reasons. Society will be better served, these liberationists maintain, if individuals, regardless of their sex, are not denied the chance to develop their potential, whatever it may be, in areas of work and play that have little or nothing to do with the basic differences between men and women, boys and girls. While a great many people still see men's and women's liberation as an attempt to homogenize the sexes, the goal in fact is to base gender distinctions firmly on the imperative differences instead of on culturally prescribed work and play differences that penalize a great many individuals but no longer serve any societal purpose, and in most instances now actually run counter to society's best interests.

Youth Pioneers

Young pioneers are breaking through the barriers of secrecy, taboo, and ignorance to seek suitable ways of managing their sex lives during the lengthening period between attainment of sexual maturity and marriage. They are rebelling against the tremendous pressure put on them to marry and start reproducing whether they are ready to or not, and against a system that insists they choose a partner for this enterprise, which is supposed to last a lifetime, without any chance of finding out much about him or her sexually and erotically.

The pressure to marry turns every encounter between a young man and a young woman into a test of the other as a potential husband or wife. Hope of using the other to escape the frowned-upon single state, and wariness lest the other exploit one as a means to his or her own escape, make it all but impossible for them to approach each other honestly. Economics further distorts their view of each other. A system that makes a man financially responsible for the woman he dates and the woman he marries, and which ties a woman's social and financial status to getting a husband, makes competition, manipulation, and exploitation an inevitable part of dating and mating.

If a young man and woman get past those hurdles, there was until recently the terrible fear of unsanctioned pregnancy to keep them from exploring their sexual compatibility before the die was cast. The fear of pregnancy has so permeated premarital relations between the sexes in American society as to constitute a form of aversion therapy. The wonder is not that sexual apathy, impotence and difficulty with orgasm afflict so many American men, or that apathy, frigidity, and anorgasmia became practically endemic among American women, but that anybody escaped such distortions.

Society, for its own protection, now grudgingly grants youth the Pill, but does little else to help young people learn how the sexes behave together sexually. Youth, perforce, must seek its own answers. Hollywood and the novelists may have given modern youngsters a better idea of where to start their sex lives than on the back seat of a car or in a sleazy motel, but not much idea about how, and most of that misleading. The following excerpt from the files of John Early III (personal communication), who is preparing a book on the subject, shows what can be expected at one level of society when the blind are left to lead the blind into the mysteries of sexual intercourse.

At the age of seventeen, the desire to lose my virginity became an obsession. I left for a vacation at Cape Cod, accompanied by my best friend who was almost as intent at losing his virginity as I was. I came back and my virginity did also, for I had met the most beautiful, sexy, intelligent girl in the world, fell sickly in love for two days, and that was it, for she went home. During the time I was with that girl I don't think I had a sexual thought. The cause? It was the old double standard of the girl I'll screw versus the girl I'll marry, or put another way, "There won't be many virgins left when I get done, but my wife damn well better be."

I entered a latency period for ten months, pining away over this girl, but spring came and I was tired of masturbating and once again I decided that I should go out and get the real thing. So I ventured forth and tangled horns with Linda, a good-looking, first-generation Italian girl, kept in the house and not allowed to date by an overprotective mother who was just off the boat. She allowed Linda to date me, for I was Italian — half-Italian at least — and what's more I was going to be a doctor, so her mother guessed it would be all right. So after saying one Our Father and two Hail Marys, she consented to us going out. Well, the first time we went to a movie, and the second time we went to the woods, and the third time we went to the woods. It turned out that Linda was a very aggressive girl, a quality which I've since grown to appreciate. At the time, I didn't.

When we went to the woods it was a warm spring night. I brought a blanket, a bottle of wine, and we had a cozy campfire, just like in the movies. Everything was set. I guess I'll have to admit that her breasts were the first I'd ever touched, excluding my mother's when I was a baby. I feel embarrassed giving details like this, but in the interest of science and letting you know where I was in the sex game, I guess you could say that I made it to second base and was rounding toward third when I was sent back to second by a moral code which caused her to grab the reins of her runaway hormonal horse.

On our second woods date, we modified the rules in the interest of alleviating horniness. This time we could reach third base (in her pants for all you nonsports fans) but while attempting to steal home, the ball game was rained out. The next pitch was in the form of fellatio. Impotence struck. There I was being fellatioed, or fileted, I should say, as the bone was removed. Yessiree, the ills of mankind struck. It didn't happen all at once; rather, it was a gradual deactivation. First I wondered why I was not coming, as this was purportedly one of the most erotic acts one could engage in. I thought about the sexiest pornography I'd ever viewed, I relived the greatest sexual fantasies I'd ever masturbated to. Then I really began to worry, and then — limp dick! What it all came down to — no pun intended — was that I simply turned off. I ended up with a badly bruised ego and a badly bruised glans penis, as

Linda had no idea of the sensitive nature of that part of the anatomy. Linda and I packed up and drove home and that was the last date we ever had. It was a strange ride, for while I didn't want her to think I was impotent, I kept my mouth shut because I didn't want to risk making her feel like a failure as a woman. It turns out that each of us was thinking, There's something wrong with me, but we didn't say a word.

That summer enter Anne, a wonderful girl and also a virgin. One night we got involved to the point of having sexual intercourse. Picture the situation. I'm with a person I love and am ridding myself of my albatross of virginity, and thoroughly enjoying it. It was a supreme experience; in fact, it was too good to be true. After ejaculating post coitus interruptus to protect her, I was told that there had been no coitus to be interrupted. She was still a virgin and the whole process turned out to have been a spillage of seed, for I had never been inside her. You must realize that having never been in a vagina before, I was not in much of a position to judge what one felt like. I went downstairs and had a can of grape soda to settle my nerves. We can laugh today, in fact it has become a standing joke between us that I don't even know when I'm screwing someone.

Now for the climax you've been waiting for: boy meets girl and loses virginity. Shelley and I developed a relationship of two people equally intent upon losing their virginities. This time things were different. She went to Planned Parenthood and got the Pill, so that was all right. When we attempted to have intercourse, I was so ready to go that I engaged in about twenty seconds of foreplay before attempting intromission, at which she exclaimed, "Gene, you can't just screw me!" Those words stung. I sort of knew that foreplay was important, but really hadn't much idea of how long. All sorts of complications then developed, and you must realize that I was standing on a very thin piece of the ice of confidence, ready to crash through at any moment.

The first complication was her lack of vaginal lubrication. I didn't know how to deal with it, so she suggested Vaseline. This wasn't too smart, for as I now know, petroleum jelly not only dissolves the rubber of a condom, which wasn't a consideration then, but also gums up female plumbing. Then I engaged in manual stimulation, whereupon she gasped that I was rubbing her raw. I attempted intromission again, but she was so tight it was impossible. I thought I was doing something wrong, and she thought she was doing something wrong. We both lay back in disgust, silent. But then I summoned up the courage to say that, in case she hadn't already noticed, I didn't know what I was doing. She admitted that she didn't either. It was a big revelation to us both, and from then on things went better.

The key point to these disasters was ignorance. Linda didn't know that stabbing me in the penis with pencilpoint fingernails was not, for me, an erotic experience, or that her ungentle oral attentions were more like a nightmare. How could she know that a penis is not a ceramic? No one had ever told her. With Linda, I didn't know much about impotence or what can cause it, all I knew was that you were less of a man if it happened to you. The major problem with Anne was general ignorance of the mechanics of the act. Another problem was my complete ignorance of the aspects of contraception. Coitus interruptus, good God! I didn't know that simple intromission can be enough to cause a pregnancy, and I certainly didn't know that you have to have the reflexes of a log-rolling champion to pull out at the right time.

With Shelley, I didn't know why foreplay was necessary, knew nothing of the components leading to orgasm or how to get someone there, and I practically wore out her clitoris, for its sensitivity was unknown to me. In fact, what I and my partners knew about sex was incomplete, from watching the great studs perform as lovers, on the movie screen. We were never told that sexual proficiency is a learned thing, not an innate reflex.

The depressing thing about these reminiscences is that all the grief was so totally unnecessary. Our hero won through, but think how easily he could have been stuck forever in the ranks of men whose sex lives are so drab that they — and their wives — can't understand what all the excitement is about. Different versions of the same story can be found in different social strata.

Today many adolescent boys and girls are sharing beds, rooms, apartments, and houses, sometimes only for a day or two, sometimes for years. Ross V. Speck, a Philadelphia psychiatrist and youth advocate, reported in a television panel discussion on February 7, 1974, that in his city alone there are now some five thousand communes. While the first ones were formed by dropouts and addicts, most of those today are what Speck calls respectable.

Universities and colleges are responding to this trend by desegregating dormitories. According to *Time* magazine (June 3, 1974), more than half of the country's resident college students now live in mixed-sex buildings. A survey of women students at Radcliffe College (Reid, 1974) found that the shift to coed dorms there had not increased the incidence of casual sex. What the survey found increased was the incidence of long-term love affairs, of enduring platonic friendships with men, and of friendship and respect between the women. A decrease was noted in the self-consciousness of the women students when they were with men and in their preoccupation with men.

There is plenty of evidence that youth is seeking not sex per se but more satisfactory forms of relationships between the sexes that center around sex. Even John Early's erotic beginner, with the avowed purpose of simply losing his virginity, found it impossible to accomplish that matter-of-fact objective until he and Shelley felt secure enough with each other to talk about their feelings. The shift in relationships is not away from commitment, but away from conventional forms of commitment toward interpersonal commitment, from "What will people say?"

to "What will my partner feel?" about the way a relationship is handled.

Early in the century strictly interpersonal commitments were not recognized at all. A commitment was undertaken by announcing a formal engagement, usually late in adolescence, followed by a long engagement period and marriage. Whatever happened to the feelings of the engaged couple during the interval, to break an engagement was a disgrace. Then the exchange of class rings or club pins became a commitment that was recognized in one's immediate circle of acquaintanceship but promised nothing to society in general. To "unpin" created only a limited social stir. There was still a formal engagement, a promise to society to marry and stay married, but the engagement period grew shorter and eventually practically disappeared. Next "going steady" became the custom. Going steady promised society that a couple had a reasonable expectation that they would become engaged and marry, but it could be abandoned without any need to explain to any but close friends and companions. Going steady then relaxed into an even more personal commitment, promising others only that the couple intended to stay together for some indefinite length of time, with no presumption that it carried any outside obligation as a prelude to anything more permanent.

Today's youth pioneers are more likely to set up housekeeping together without inviting society to take any notice at all and with marriage in mind themselves only as a possible future contingency.

Perhaps the thrust of the youth pioneers can best be read as an attack on the ancient dichotomy between love (ennobling) and lust (degrading), a phony distinction which has poisoned relations between the sexes for so long. A man who has been taught from infancy that sexual advances are an insult to women has little choice but to seek his sexual pleasure either with men or with women he feels are degraded enough to be insulted safely. What kind of relations with women can a man have if, like many Victorians, he screws at a whorehouse and then goes home to worship his wife? The dichotomy between love and lust mandates distortion of sexuality.

One typical kind of distortion is to depersonalize eroticism by focusing on a fetish. Another is sadomasochism, as illustrated by a couple who recently came to Johns Hopkins for treatment. Outside of their bedroom these two would be on anybody's list of normal suburban couples, but as treatment progressed it developed that the only way he could be sexually aroused was for her to tie him up, threaten and beat him, tell him she was a whore, and force orgasm upon him. The difficulty of getting love and lust together again after they have been firmly severed in childhood is at the root of almost every problem of erotic relations between two people. Not only heterosexuals but homosexuals demonstrate this very clearly; they find it hard to establish sexual relations with members of the other sex and in many instances equally hard to establish lasting friendships with members of their own sex with whom they have sexual relationships. You might say that the basic problem is getting heads and tails together in the same relationship. Conversely, heterosexuals may find it easy to establish sexual relations with the opposite sex but not the kind of lasting friendships that they expect to have with members of their own sex.

At first the emphasis of the youth pioneers was on taking the curse off lust, establishing their right to physical intimacy without shame. They borrowed the earlier terms "shacking up," "girlfriend," and "boyfriend." As the aim broadens, they are using terms like "living friend," or simply "friend," meaning "someone I live with and care for" without specifying whether the friend is male or female or whether or not the relationship is based on sexual intimacy. Whereas young couples who walk with their arms entwined, perhaps stopping now and then to kiss, once meant to advertise that they were sexual lovers, they now, as likely as not, mean to advertise affection and support for each other without implying whether they are or are not sexually involved.

Inevitably those who have been taught that lust is degrading view attempts to abolish the false dichotomy as downgrading love. Logically, according to this view, love finds its fullest expression in physical castration, as has been practiced by some religious sects, notably the Russian Skoptsy and a few of the early Christians, or the functional castration of celibacy, as practiced by the Shaker sect and vowed by Roman Catholic priests to this day. Since the human race is not bent on species suicide, however, the definition of love has always been stretched to include sex as essential to procreation, even when its recreational aspects were being damned as lust. Now that contraception makes it possible to separate recreational from procreational sex entirely, this legacy makes it hard to admit any connection between recreational sex and love.

The fact is that sex play and procreation both have significance for human health and well-being, and each provides opportunities for emotional investment — love. If one person is your only partner in both procreation and sex play, your chance of loving that person is greater and your chance of a greater love is increased, but it doesn't necessarily mean that you *will* love that person or that your love for him or her will be more intense than if you had other partners. Nor is it necessary to assume that the significance of either recreational or procreational sex is lessened by separating them. Furthermore, however much love unquestionably enriches both recreational and procreational sex, the truth is that love is not essential to either. Sex without love is quite adequate for procreation, and casual sexual encounters can be rewarding simply for their own sake.

The conditions that made intensive procreation necessary nourished the convention that sex without love is fun for men but not for women. This convention, backed by the possibility of pregnancy and the economic hamstringing of women, led to the oneupsmanship games of incessantly-horny-boy-maneuvers-always-reluctant-girl-into-bed, girl-entraps-boy-into-marriage, and their variants, which the youth pioneers are refusing to play. What the convention obscured is that there have always been some women who could enjoy casual recreational sex and some men who could not. With reliable contraception and the gradual economic enfranchisement of women, the stereotypes have begun to ease on this score, and as the stereotypes become more flexible, the ratio of men and women who enjoy casual recreational sex may well change.

Today we can afford to admit the possibility that sex play, divorced from both procreation and love, may be what a lot of people — many of them intelligent and highly ethical — have always maintained it was: a positive good, a healthy sport. When recreational sex could not be separated from procreation, society had a right to demand that those who engaged in sex play be prepared to accept the adult responsibilities of parenthood. Contraception means that society need demand only that those who are not prepared to accept the responsibilities of parenthood take care not to become parents. If sex partners do this, their responsibility is only to themselves and each other. What they need from society is the information, guidance, and opportunity to gain the experience that will enable them to understand their own and their partners' sexuality.

Another legacy youth pioneers are assaulting is the prescription for the duration of sexual relationships. The assumption that any decent sexual relationship must last for the rest of your life puts far too heavy a burden on the early stages of any relationship, especially one of adolescents, with their earlier puberty and lengthening life expectancy. One way of acknowledging depth and intensity in a relationship without being stuck forever, if it fades, is to practice serial monogamy via the divorce court. Those who attribute most of society's present ills to broken homes, and blame the rising divorce rate, forget that a hundred years ago the rate of broken homes due to death roughly equaled the rate of broken homes due to divorce today. Nevertheless, the inequities of the divorce laws and the hypocrisy that permeates divorce proceedings in most jurisdictions make divorce an inordinately destructive solution to the problem of duration, and society is at long last beginning to look for better solutions. One alternative that has been proposed is a three-year marriage contract, renewable or dissolvable at term, which would have the highly desirable effect of encouraging only high-quality unions to endure and allowing poor ones to lapse of inertia without the trauma of divorce. What effect pregnancy or the arrival of children should have on such contracts is an important point, but it's hard to escape the conclusion that people who marry because they want to have children together will make a better family unit than people who marry because it is the only way they can get permission to enjoy each other sexually.

The youth pioneers won a measure of tolerance from society after the costly rebellions of the 1960s, but tolerance is not enough. Permissiveness can quickly degenerate into guilt-ridden irresponsibility, and new stereotypes can be as stultifying as the old. They need the wisest, most sympathetic help society can give them, for so often, as George Bach and Ronald Deutsch (1970) point out in their book, *Pairing,*

Despite their honest effort, most of the rebels manage to cultivate only the outward semblances of the intimacy they seek. The closeness, the authenticity, the transparency, the freedom of expression of intimate love eludes them. Instead they manage only an ersatz intimacy — with emphasis on public nudity, partner-swapping and an occasional orgy. Their "candor" is only a shadow — of four-letter words, self-pitying confessions, amateur psychoanalysis and encounter, and blunt attack on others in the name of honesty.

Old Age Pioneers

The strident demands of adolescents for a timely beginning of their sex lives are finding an echo in timid complaints from the elderly against the untimely ending of theirs. Faint protests against segregation of the sexes and lack of privacy for couples can sometimes be heard in old-age colonies and nursing homes across the land, if anybody stops to listen.

Society's refusal to accept the idea that sex can be important after fifty or sixty can be traced to many sources, most of them invalid. It is also easy to find reasons why oldsters are hesitant about voicing their complaints, but that, too, is changing.

Nobody bothered to inquire into geriatric sex much in the past because until recently most people didn't expect to reach that stage of life. As long as elderly people were few and far between, their needs were handled, for good or ill, on an ad hoc basis. But the generation that produced the baby boom found itself with a geriatric boom on its hands as well, thanks in good part to the antibiotics developed during World War II. In 1940 there were nine million people over sixty-four years old in the United States; today there are twenty million, almost 10 percent of the population. This population shift created a lot of problems, few of which have yet been solved. Geriatric sexuality is only one of those problems, and it is far down the list for the families, old-age home personnel and doctors who are trying to cope, and for the oldsters themselves. In fact it's hardly on the list at all, since most people still assume that the erotic turn-on promptly turns off in women at menopause and in men by the time they reach sixty. Speculation about the motives of those who marry late in life seldom includes the possibility that physical sexual attraction inspired the match.

There are, of course, plenty of people whose sexual interest and capabilities do fade with age, and there are those who gladly use aging as an excuse to avoid the sexual encounters they never enjoyed anyway. Nevertheless, a number of studies, notably those of Kinsey, the Duke University Center for the Study of Aging, and Masters and Johnson, have firmly disproved the idea that sex is either impossible or abnormal for people past the age of sixty, seventy, eighty, or even ninety. In its studies of aging over the past twenty years, the Duke center has found that sexual interest actually increased with age in about 15 percent of the men and women who have served as subjects there. In an experiment at the Mount Sinai Hospital Sleep Laboratory in New York, psychiatrist Charles Fisher found that most of his twenty-one subjects, all men over seventy, had penile erections with their sexual dreaming, including one man who was ninety-six years old. Nor is it particularly rare for a woman to become orgasmic for the first time in her life only after menopause has banished fear of pregnancy.

There are other fears to replace the fear of pregnancy as sex inhibitors for the elderly. The fear that sexual intercourse may precipitate a medical disaster such as a heart attack is one. Jokes and the publicity given to the rare occurrences have increased such fears out of all proportion. When the danger is real, there are often ways to reduce it to an acceptable risk, but the old people who could extend their sex lives if they had proper medical advice seldom get it. Like the rest of society, doctors tend to discount geriatric sexuality, although to ignore the older patient's sex life is poor medical practice. Besides gladdening the patient's life, sexual activity is good therapy, as Robert N. Butler (Butler and Lewis, 1973) and others have been telling the medical profession. "For one thing, sex can relieve psychological tension," Butler explained, in a personal communication,

and for another, it can increase the cortisone output of the adrenal glands, which is a help in conditions like arthritis. Then, too, a good deal of needless anxiety would be avoided if it were generally known, for example, that removing a man's prostate doesn't usually make him impotent, but how many people know it? A lot of doctors don't know these things, and some of those who do know never bother to tell their older patients because they think sex doesn't matter to them.

Along with the rest of society, old people themselves find it hard to believe in geriatric sexuality. Having subscribed to the stereotypical view all their lives, many are too shocked at the discovery that their sexual feelings persist to admit such "depravity," even to themselves, much less to complain about a home that gives them no opportunity to indulge such feelings, whether they are living with younger relatives or in a community run for the elderly.

For an old person to announce wedding plans is to ask for derisive comments or for the surprise and overeffusiveness that is a cover for embarrassment. If the elderly bride or groom has children who sense a threat to their inheritance, it may be asking for worse. The sons of a gentle (and wealthy) California lady, who radiated happiness when she remarried at seventy, took their mother bodily away from her septuagenarian husband and never allowed her to see him again. Such reactions, plus the practical consideration that remarriage often reduces pensions and Social Security benefits, are driving old people to live quietly "in sin." In spite of the reluctance to defy convention that is ingrained in most of them, more and more oldsters are emulating the young by simply moving in together without legal or social formalities. Even that isn't always safe, for there are people who have tried to commit a parent to a mental institution on the grounds that an old person's wish to live with a member of the opposite sex is evidence of mental derangement! A small but growing number of the elderly are now establishing communes where they make their own rules.

What old people need from society is what young people need, help in understanding their sexuality and opportunities to enjoy it under decent conditions. Sexuality is as significant in old age as in youth, even for those whose capacity for sexual intercourse has been impaired. Could you tell from this letter, for example, that the writer is in her seventies?

My darling: I can't get over the shock of realizing that you don't love me, at least not enough for us to live together. For so long now you've been all I thought about and lived for and planned for, and I know you know that I took this place so we could live here together. The best thing for me to do is go away. As long as I'm here, I know I'll always be haunted by my foolish dreams and memories of you. You asked me why we can't just go on the way we are, and the answer is that I need your closeness, and need to know without any doubt that I am loved. I want you to touch me and hold me in your arms in the morning as well as in the evening. I remember the times you've put your hand on my shoulder for no reason when I was reading, or leaned against me while we listened to music, or kissed my ear as I arranged the flowers. Those are the things that make me feel like a woman and make life worthwhile, even more than sex.

Married Pioneers

In the various camps of the married pioneers, the underlying goal is to stretch the cultural stereotype of marriage, which was designed mainly as a framework for the growth and development of children, into a better framework for the growth and development of the marriage partners. The goal grows progressively more desirable as procreation fills less and less of the horizon between sexual maturity and the grave.

Protest focuses on society's demand for sexual fidelity to the spouse and the double standard of enforcing the requirement. Such protest is as old as monogamy, but has gained momentum from the industrial revolution and the women's liberation movement that has grown in pace with that revolution. Sexual fidelity, say the protesters, should be voluntary; forcing it is destructive of marriage because it makes too many spouses choose between sexual bondage on the one hand and hypocrisy and deceit on the other. "We have so strenuously inculcated this romantic fiction into the young couple," Havelock Ellis wrote of monogamic marriage back in 1928, "that when they privately discover that it is a fiction, they are overwhelmed with a sense of personal guilt, and only in rare instances dare to confide in each other and to attain that mutual sincerity and trust which might well be regarded as in itself, even in the absence of sexual fidelity, the finest form of marriage" (Ellis, 1952). With less restraint, James and Lynn Smith wrote in the introduction to the book *Beyond Monogamy* (1974), "The monogamic code [that one forsake all others] is so antisocial and contrary to human nature that an entire social ideology and an assortment of socially engineered pretenses and excuses have been devised to avoid and evade it."

The more conservative married pioneers don't actually advocate extramarital sex relations, but discount fidelity except as it grows naturally out of the partners' allegiance and feelings for each other. Nena and George O'Neill (1972) defined this position at length:

We have no intention, of course, of denying that some people *can* be sexually monogamous for life. Some couples can and do achieve a union in which neither one ever has or even wants extramarital liaisons. But they are rare, and becoming rarer. . . . The guidelines throughout this book are dedicated to redefining monogamy, to creating a kind of monogamy in which equality naturally exists and identity flourishes, in which jealousy and sexual exclusivity become beside the point, in which decisions are made by choice, not coercion, and love grows in a climate of freedom.

At the other extreme are the "swingers," who arrange a sex game with another couple or a sex party with a group as an expected part of their social life. Like a card game or a cocktail party, they see it as a way of entertaining their friends and extending their acquaintanceship among people of similar tastes. It is a rule of etiquette with many of these groups that they keep their emotional commitment and allegiance inside their marriages.

In between the conservatives and the swingers are those whose objective is to expand their emotional development, using sex as one way of extending their emotional commitments beyond the marriage. Among them are those who adopt an extra partner or partners into the marriage relationship or set up conjugal relations with another couple or couples.

Lynn Smith put the case for swinging strongly in her 1973 doctoral dissertation for the University of California at Berkeley. "Comarital involvement is, if nothing else and most basically, a learning experience. It 'moves' the individual. It provides an opportunity and a challenge to explore one's sexual desires, sexual needs, sexual responses, one's belief system and self-concept." Only timidity, she implies, would keep a person back.

Such a challenging, of course, carries risks, but they are the inevitable risks of exploring reality and oneself. It may be safer to back away, to retreat from such a challenge and opt for the status quo, without further exploring its reality and without challenging its illusions. Sometimes we feel we need illusions to accept ourselves. But then sometimes we short-change ourselves and do ourselves a disservice.

In their five years of research on swinging, the Smiths have discerned a tendency on the part of those who start out playing consensual adultery as an antidote to conventional adultery, as a game or sport that excludes emotional involvement, to shift over a period of time into concern with interpersonal relations. "One is tempted to suggest that a maturational process occurs," they conclude. They may be right, but it is a common observation that many people lose interest in a penny-ante poker game unless the stakes build up to a point where they have significance for the players. It may be that swingers add emotional investment to the stakes in their games in order to maintain their interest in playing. Another possible interpretation of this shift is that once swingers exorcise the idea that lust is degrading, they then feel impelled to put love and lust together in their relationships with other swingers.

Those who regard the married pioneers as sick haven't yet made any sort of case. On the contrary, none of the studies completed so far has yielded evidence of any more psychopathology among participants than among their conventional counterparts. Nor is there any evidence that the children of married pioneers suffer as a result of the pioneering unless the children are penalized by society's disapproval of their parents' activities.

Contraception makes it possible for us and our society to consider our attitude toward marriage and procreation entirely apart from our attitude toward recreational sex. To do so does not necessarily downgrade marriage. In fact, it is more logical to assume that such separation would go a long way toward improving family life. Since even the most strenuous efforts to confine recreational sex within the limits of permanent marriage have never been notably effective, is the effort worth the price in hypocrisy and family friction? The married pioneers say no. As for their children, comarital involvement can offer them at least some of the advantages of the extended family, depending, of course, on how the involvement is managed. And where strict fidelity is a strain on a marriage, easing that strain could well make it easier for a couple to see their parental responsibilities more clearly and take more pleasure in fulfilling them.

Single Adult Pioneers

Little need be said here about the single adult pioneers, partly because their goals are similar to those of the youth pioneers that have been considered in detail, and partly because they have so largely achieved their main goal of sexual freedom in the cities and increasingly in the suburbs and smaller communities as well.

While the principle of fair play applies to all sexual relations, this may be a good place to point out that it is the essence of any game or sport that the players understand and abide by the rules of the game. When the generally understood rules set by the stereotypes are abandoned, it is important that the partners in a sexual relationship understand each other. If they don't, somebody is liable to be seriously hurt. Single adults owe it to themselves and each other to establish at the start of a relationship whether they regard it as a brief encounter or a commitment of whatever sort. The rules can be changed as you go along, of course, but it shouldn't be done unilaterally without notice. For some people this is all easier said than done, like the nude swimming and sunbathing on public beaches that is blossoming into sudden popularity.

8.   The Road Ahead

MANY OF THE PIONEERS maintain that stereotyped differences between the sexes should be done away with, and many nonpioneers fear that relaxing gender stereotypes will do away with all differences and homogenize the sexes. Both groups are tilting at windmills. As long as there is a human race, there almost certainly will be differences between the sexes in sexual behavior, work, and play. The theme of this book is that sex differences are relative, not absolute. They can be assigned however we wish, as long as we allow for two simple facts: first, that men impregnate, women menstruate, gestate, and lactate; and second, that adult individuals cannot alter the nuclear core of their gender schemas.

Once a sex distinction has worked or been pressured

into the nuclear core of your gender schema, to dislodge it is to threaten you as an individual with destruction. The gate is as firmly locked there as it is on your chromosomes and gonads. If you're a man with trousers bound deep in the core of your male schema, you will be as uncomfortable in a skirt, even if it's a traditional male kilt, as you would be if you developed voluptuous breasts. If you're a woman with passive dependence bound deep in the core of your female schema, you will be as uncomfortable wielding authority as if you grew a full beard. People can no more be expected to decode behavior that has been locked into the core of their gender schemas than a Chinese woman whose feet were bound in childhood could be expected to walk naturally. What you can be expected to do is to recognize that such limitations are not a law of nature, and that society, and your own children, may be better served by different kinds of sex distinctions than the ones you have incorporated.

For you as a member of society, the challenge is to help bring more flexibility into the cultural stereotypes so that those who are growing up today need not be handicapped by having obsolete sex distinctions driven into the core of their gender schemas by the pressure of stereotypes that are unnecessarily rigid. Although whole libraries have been written about the dynamics of cultural change, the process is still not very well understood. Nevertheless it is a process familiar to all of us. One example, the trivial matter of hair length, shows how gender stereotypes become more flexible.

Early in the century, long hair was a rigid feature of the female gender stereotype. The longer the hair, the more feminine the woman, and the femininity of a woman who wore her hair short was automatically called into

231

question. (The masculinity of a man who wore his hair long was also open to question for a brief while, despite the fact that the history and geography books, churches and halls of fame abounded with portrayals of unquestionably masculine men with flowing tresses.) After enough women had experimented with bobbed hair to blunt this feature of the female stereotype, bobbed hair became the female norm, although it was not as rigid a feature of the stereotype as long hair had been. But by the time the stereotype relaxed, long hair was already deeply embedded in the schemas of many older women, and they continued to wear their hair long. Note that while some of the women's styles were called boy-cuts, very few women actually had their hair cut man-fashion. Jokes and dire predictions notwithstanding, bobbed hair didn't blur sex differences a whit. Today most young women are again wearing their hair long, and it's mainly older women who cut theirs short, but this feature of the gender stereotype is so flexible that no one would think of questioning a woman's femininity on the basis of her hair style.

When, later in the century, young men started letting their hair grow long, you'd have thought from the public outcry that they'd invented some new kind of perversion. That, too, has become flexible and today a man can go cropped and clean-shaven or shaggy as a sheep dog without exciting speculation about his masculinity. Psychiatrist Povl Toussieng (1970) described the flexing of his own reactions to hair length as an index of masculinity as he once watched a group of adolescents "doing" each others' hair while they sunbathed around a swimming pool. At first he assumed the boys were effeminate, but as it happened, they started teasing one of their number about having been approached by a homosexual, and the banter made it quite clear that everybody in the group knew very well that this boy was not in the least homosexual. "He was a well-built and quite muscular young man," Toussieng reported,

something I had failed to notice when I merely observed his girlish way of handling his locks. It was obvious to me now that the girls and boys were indeed reacting to each other as boys and girls, but in a novel, more subtle and far more differentiated way than I had ever before observed in youngsters this age. Particularly worth noting was the degree of camaraderie and relaxation they showed with each other. There was not the slightest trace of the kinds of boisterous, exhibitionistic and teasingly aggressive games in which previous generations of young teenagers used to engage in order to cope with their heterosexual anxiety. Most impressive of all was the openness and comfort with which these youngsters talked to each other about intimate subjects.

The length of scalp hair is an arbitrary matter, and other sex distinctions are far more in need of reassessment. No societal purpose is served by coding hair length either way, except that there must be sex differences so that when more reliable distinctions are obscured, things like hair length acquire rigidity in order to provide a substitute. But if society or your early environment drove that distinction into the core of your gender schema so that it has become an integral support for your gender identity, society has no right to demand that you now drive it out again. And if your fate or society made you a homosexual, transvestite or transexual, society cannot fairly penalize you for being what you are. Survival today calls for far more flexibility and tolerance of experimentation than has yet been achieved; overpopulation, longevity, contraception, and technology mean that we can afford it.

Society lost nothing when the female stereotype was stretched to accommodate tomboy girls. The test girls of Chapter 3 are no more of a threat to society than the control girls, and they are certainly happier, healthier, and more productive than if they had been forced to suppress their energies and redirect their natural bent. Society can equally well afford to stretch the male stereotype to accommodate quiet, sensitive boys and men, without stigmatizing them as effeminate.

For our society today, the challenge is to reaffirm the genital and reproductive differences between the sexes as the foundation of the gender stereotypes, to decode into the human stereotype the sex distinctions of the past that have become straitjackets, and to keep the rest of the gender stereotypes flexible enough to meet present and future change.

Decoding a particular feature of the stereotype or making it more flexible doesn't bring flexibility into the gender schemas of individuals immediately. For example, the stereotype has been easing up for several generations on the sex-coding of vocations that for ages were embedded deep in the male stereotype. Old men whose schemas were set before the stereotype relaxed still find it hard to accept women as office colleagues, members of the board, police officers, taxi drivers, and so forth, but young men take it in stride and no longer feel their masculinity threatened. Middle-aged men like the psychiatrist in Chapter 5 feel uncomfortable sharing the daily labor and rewards of running a home and rearing children, whereas many young men are indignant when these are denied them — and so on.

For you as a parent, or teacher, or simply as a member of society, the challenge is to help those who are growing up today to understand and build their gender schemas firmly on the genital and reproductive differences between the sexes, and to keep the rest of their schemas flexible.

You as an individual must, of course, protect the nuclear core of your gender schemas. You can, however, distinguish between the nuclear core and the flexible part, and keep your schemas as flexible as possible. You can remind yourself that except for the basic four, the core parts of your schemas, which you yourself cannot afford to decode, are not divinely ordained eternal verities; they differentiated over a period of years in the interaction between your particular nature and your particular nurture, which may be similar to but are not identical with those of the rest of your society. Sexual behavior that would be destructive for you is not necessarily wrong for your neighbor.

You can temper your attitude toward your fellow men and women with tolerance, recognizing that relaxation of the gender stereotypes offers you the chance to enjoy life more not just as *a* man or *a* woman, but as the special kind of man or woman that you are and can be.

More than ever before in human history, we today can afford to relate to each other as human beings and as individuals instead of strictly as males and females. To the extent that we can broaden our human schemas and prune our gender schemas back, sex differences will flourish in far greater variety. Far from blurring the differences between the sexes, freeing ourselves from stale, repetitive, artificially imposed patterns of difference will allow the real differences to emerge. The more of his individual self a man can develop without having to question his masculinity, the more of her individual self a woman can develop without having to question her femininity, the more of a person each can be, and the more fully they can complement and enhance each other. Surely there's no joy in a prescribed response to another individual that compares with the joy of discovering one's own unique ability to complement and enhance one's unique partner. There are glorious possibilities of manhood and womanhood to be explored beyond the stereotypic "If you're a man you must" and "If you're a woman you must" barriers that the accelerating rate of change and the sexual revolution are sweeping away.

Bibliography

Bach, G. R., and Deutsch, R. M. 1970. *Pairing: A Psychologist Shows How to Achieve Genuine Intimacy.* New York, Peter H. Wyden. Paperback edition, Avon.

Benjamin, H. 1966. *The Transsexual Phenomenon.* New York, Julian Press.

Broverman, I. K.; Broverman, D. M.; Clarkson, F. E.; Rosenkrantz, P. S.; and Vogel, S. R. 1970. "Sex-Role Stereotypes and Clinical Judgments of Mental Health." *Journal of Consulting and Clinical Psychology* 34:1–7.

Butler, R. N., and Lewis, M. I. 1973. *Aging and Mental Health: Positive Psychosocial Approaches.* St. Louis, C. V. Mosby.

Comfort, A., ed. 1972. *The Joy of Sex: A Cordon Bleu Guide to Lovemaking.* New York, Crown.

Cowell, R. E. 1954. *Roberta Cowell's Story.* London, W. Heinemann; New York, British Book Centre.

Ellis, H. 1952. *Sex and Marriage.* New York, Random House. Paperback edition, Pyramid.

Farb, P. 1974. *Word Play: What Happens When People Talk.* New York, Alfred A. Knopf.

Farrell, W. 1974. *The Liberated Man: Beyond Masculinity — Free-*

237

ing Men and Their Relationships with Women. New York, Random House.

Ferracuti, F. 1972. "Incest Between Father and Daughter." In H. L. P. Resnik and M. E. Wolfgang, eds., *Sexual Behaviors: Social, Clinical, and Legal Aspects.* Boston, Little, Brown.

Flynn, L. B. 1972. "The Hardy Boys Didn't Have Wet Dreams." *SIECUS Report* 1(2):1–2. New York, Sex Information and Education Council of the U.S.

Goldberg, P. 1968. "Are Women Prejudiced Against Other Women?" *Trans-Action* 5(5):28–30. St. Louis, Washington University.

Karlen, A. 1971. *Sexuality and Homosexuality: A New View.* New York, W. W. Norton.

Laird, C. 1953. *The Miracle of Language.* Cleveland, World.

Mead, M. 1949. *Male and Female: A Study of the Sexes in a Changing World.* New York, William Morrow. Paperback edition, New American Library Mentor book.

Money, J. 1968. *Sex Errors of the Body.* Baltimore, Johns Hopkins University Press.

———. 1973a. "Gender Role, Gender Identity, Core Gender Identity: Usage and Differentiation of Terms." *Journal of the American Academy of Psychoanalysis* 1:397–403.

———. 1973b. "Pornography in the Home: A Topic in Medical Education." In J. Zubin and J. Money, eds., *Contemporary Sexual Behavior: Critical Issues in the 1970s.* Baltimore, Johns Hopkins University Press.

———. 1974. "Prenatal Hormones and Postnatal Sexualization in Gender Identity Differentiation." In J. K. Cole and R. Dienstbier, eds., *Nebraska Symposium on Motivation.* Lincoln, University of Nebraska Press.

Money, J., and Ehrhardt, A. 1972. *Man & Woman Boy & Girl: The Differentiation and Dimorphism of Gender Identity from Conception to Maturity.* Baltimore, Johns Hopkins University Press. Paperback edition, Johns Hopkins University Press.

Money, J.; Hampson, J. G.; and Hampson, J. L. 1955. "Hermaphroditism: Recommendations Concerning Assignment of Sex, Change of Sex, and Psychologic Management." *Bulletin of The Johns Hopkins Hospital* 97: 284–300.

Morris, J. 1974. *Conundrum.* New York, Harcourt Brace Jovanovich.

Nixon, E. 1965. *Royal Spy: The Strange Case of the Chevalier D'Eon.* New York, Reynal.

O'Neill, N., and O'Neill, G. 1972. *Open Marriage: A New Life Style for Couples.* New York, M. Evans.

Petrie, A. 1967. *Individuality in Pain and Suffering.* Chicago, University of Chicago Press.

Price, D. 1972. "Mammalian Conception, Sex Differentiation, and Hermaphroditism as Viewed in Historical Perspective." *American Zoologist* 12:179–91.

Reid, E. A. 1974. "Effects of Coresidential Living on the Attitudes, Self-Image, and Role Expectations of College Women." *American Journal of Psychiatry* 131:551–554.

Richter, C. P. 1965. *Biological Clocks in Medicine and Psychiatry.* Springfield, Ill., Charles C Thomas.

Robertson, D. R. 1972. "Social Control of Sex Reversal in a Coral Reef Fish." *Science* 177:1007–1009.

Rosenblatt, J. S. 1967. "Nonhormonal Basis of Maternal Behavior in the Rat." *Science* 156:1512–1514.

Schwenda, I., and Leuchner, T. 1969. *The Pictorial Guide to Sexual Intercourse.* New York (Box 1555, Grand Central Station, 10017), PENT-R Books.

Sherman, J. A. 1972. "Socializing for Maximal Female Competence." Paper presented at the annual meeting of the American Association for the Advancement of Science, Washington, D.C.

Smith, J. R., and Smith, L. G. 1974. *Beyond Monogamy: Recent Studies of Sexual Alternatives in Marriage.* Baltimore, Johns Hopkins University Press.

Stoller, R. J. 1968. *Sex and Gender: On the Development of Masculinity and Femininity.* New York, J. Aronson.

Tanner, J. M. 1962. *Growth at Adolescence,* 2nd ed. Oxford: Blackwell Scientific Publications.

Toussieng, P. 1971. "Changing Sex Roles in Changing Times." In *Sex in Childhood.* Tulsa, Children's Medical Center.

Vandenbergh, J. G. 1974. "Social Determinants of the Onset of Puberty in Rodents." *Journal of Sex Research* 10:181–193.

Westoff, C. F., and Rindfuss, R. R. 1974. "Sex Preselection in the United States: Some Implications." *Science* 184:633–636.

Wheelis, A. 1958. *The Quest for Identity.* New York, W. W. Norton.

Women on Words and Images. 1972. *Dick and Jane as Victims.* Princeton, Women on Words and Images.

Index

INDEX

Bartholomew, G. A., 171, 172
Batak people, 22–23, 165, 207
Beach, Frank, 171, 172
behavior patterns: adolescent, 153–
    154, 166–167; bisexual and ambi-
    sexual, 16, 24, 192, 206–207, 208;
    in children's games and play, 25,
    121–122, 123–128, 139, 158–159,
    184; chromosome patterns and,
    52; dominance, 79, 80–81, 97,
    199; hormones and, 80–81, 90;
    and language, 83–84; mating (of
    birds and animals), 171, 172, 173–
    175; (human), 175–176; of mon-
    keys, 74–75; parental, see parents
    and parentalism (behavior); psy-
    chosexual, 19–35, 52, 136–140;
    sex-coded or -linked, 6–7, 39, 72,
    73–75, 78–85, 120–121, 126–128,
    231–234; sex impersonations, see
    transvestism; among Vakinankara-
    tra, 83–84
Beigel, Hugo, quoted, 30
Benjamin, H., 32
Bertram, Ewart, 41
betrothal customs, 180–181, 215. See
    also mating
Bible, the, 15, 20, 25, 112, 128, 177
bicycle, invention of, 156
Biller, Henry, 205
biological clock, 154–155, 159
biological experiments with animals,
    64–68, 72, 74–75, 78
biological imperatives (reproductive
    functions), 38–40, 80, 127, 230
bipolar thinking, 15–16
birth. See childbirth; conception
birth control, 49, 176, 188–191. See
    also contraception
birth defects. See prenatal detours
birth rate and ratio. See population
bisexuality, 192, 208; ambisexuality
    and, 16, 24, 206–207
Blume, Judith, Then Again, Maybe
    I Won't, 168
brain, the; hormones and, 63–85,
    163; reptilian and limbic, 174;
    neocortex or neomammalian, 174–
    175
breast development, 40, 50, 104, 155,
    157
breast-feeding. See lactation
Broverman, Inge K., 194
Bruce, Hilda, 171, 173
"bundling," 180
Butler, Robert N., quoted, 222–223

Caligula, 25
castration, 95, 217. See also surgery
cave drawings, prehistoric, 110
celibacy, 177, 217

censorship. See pornography
Charley's Aunt (play), 34
chauvinism, sexual, 17, 79
child(ren): and childhood sexuality,
    25, 127, 134–140, 142, 166–168;
    and clothing/nudity, 129–130, 135;
    and cross-dressing, 25, 122; fan-
    tasies, 159, 166; gender identity,
    94–97, 102–108, 119–121, 125, 135,
    137–139; ignorance and misin-
    formation, 130, 140, 142, 166–167
    (see also sex education below);
    in kibbutzim, 184–185; and lan-
    guage, 82; and latent period, 121–
    140; literature for, 128, 167–168;
    molestation, 141; and parental de-
    mands and behavior, 30, 120, 121,
    124–132, 137–138, 204–205, 228;
    play, games and toys, 25, 121–
    122, 123–128, 139, 158–159, 184;
    and puberty (early), 155, 159;
    seduction period (Oedipal phase)
    of, 124, 125–126, 184; sex educa-
    tion, 128–142, 166–168; sex ex-
    ploration, 125, 128–129, 139; and
    taboos, 102–103, 132–136; and
    "unisex," 130
childbirth: children's knowledge of,
    138–139; fathers and, 161, 204
China, Red, marriage in, 159
cholesterol, 44
Christianity, 20, 84, 178, 188, 217.
    See also Bible, the; religion
chromatin spot, sex (Barr body), 42
chromosome patterns: at conception
    (XX or XY), 6, 36, 37, 41–43, 44,
    47, 50, 52–54, 59, 89; defective or
    surplus, 50, 52–54; end of influ-
    ence of, 44
Clarendon, Earl of, 25
Cleopatra, 183
cloning, 151, 170
clothing: babies and, 87; children
    and, 129–130, 135; tomboys and,
    70; and transvestism (cross-
    dressing), 19, 25, 30–31, 122; uni-
    sex, 130
coitus. See intercourse (copulation)
Comfort, Alex, The Joy of Sex, 145
commitment, 181, 214–215, 229
communes, 214
communication, 83, 109, 111, 116.
    See also language
complementation and identification,
    126–127, 142, 145
conception: children's understanding
    of, 138–139; chromosome patterns
    at, 6, 36, 41–43, 44, 47, 50, 52–
    54; limits set at, 37; and prenatal
    sex determination, 42–43

242

condoms, 43, 189. *See also* contraception

"confessions" magazines, 164

contraception: ancient, 187; availability of, 7, 169, 189–190, 193, 217–219, 228, 233; condoms, 189; the Pill, 210

copulation. *See* intercourse (copulation)

Cornbury, Lord. *See* Hyde, Edward

cortisol, 58

cortisone, 61, 101, 104, 106, 222. *See also* hormone(s)

counseling. *See* psychotherapy

courtship, 180. *See also* love and love affairs; marriage; mating

Cowell, Robert/Roberta, 90, 144; *Roberta Cowell's Story*, quoted, 33–35

crime, sex, 141–142, 165

Cromagnon people, 110

cross-dressing. *See* transvestism

Crucifixion, the, 133

cultural stereotypes: and ambisexuality, 206–207; and the elderly, 192, 221–223; and gender identity/role, 9, 10 12, 73, 130, 231 (*see also* gender stereotypes); intelligence, 81–85, 196–199, 203–204; and liberationists, 192, 229; of marriage, 224–225; modifications (flexibility) of, 148, 218, 220, 231; and society, 8–9, 10, 13, 148 (*see also* society); among Vakinankaratra, 83–84

culture(s): modern, 6–7, 37, 81; primitive, 22–23, 39, 83–84, 140, 182–185

dating and mating. *See* mating

death control. *See* life span

"degenerates" and degeneration, 165, 182–183

Denmark, sex crime rate in, 141

D'Eon, Le Chevalier/La Chevalière, 27–29

Depression, Great, 190

determination of sex. *See* differentiation, sexual; prenatal detours

Deutsch, Ronald (co-author), *Pairing*, quoted, 220

diet and puberty, 157

differentiation, sexual, 8; and Adam principle, 16, 19, 46–48, 50, 64, 66; and anatomical limits, 73–74; 127, 144; and animal experiments, 64–68, 72, 74–75, 78; and biological imperatives, 38–40, 80, 230; and intelligence, 81–85, 196–199, 203–204; and language, 109, 115–118; in "latent" period, 121–140;

and parents' role, 79–81, 126–127; and prenatal development, 44, 46–49, 81; and prenatal development errors (detours), 49–50, 52–62, 96; puberty and, 153–155, 157–158, 164–165; and "real" differences, 235–236; and reassignment (option to change), 38, 39, 72–75, 78, 81, 90–108, 119, 231; societal pressures and, 86–91, 94–97, 99–100, 233–235; and stereotypes, 10–13, 81, 130 (*see also* gender stereotypes); studies of, 6, 13–16; and within-group differences, 41

diminishers, 161

divorce, 219

dominance behavior, 79, 80–81, 97, 177, 199

Don Juan, 161

Donovan, John, *I'll Get There, It Better Be Worth the Trip*, 168

dormitories, coed, 214

double standard, 177–178, 187

dreams and fantasies, sex, 162–164, 176; of children, 159, 166; Christian religion and, 188; homosexual, 23–24

dropoutism, 109

Duke University Center for the Study of Aging, 221–222

Eagleton, Thomas, 203

Early, John, III, 214; quoted, 210–213

education, sex, 128–142, 166–168. *See also* parents and parentalism (behavior)

Edward II, king of England, 21

Egypt, ancient, 187

Ehrhardt, Anke, 9n, 18, 23, 64, 69, 165, 171, 184

Elbe, Lili (Einar Wegener), 32

Elizabeth I, queen of England, 25

Ellis, Havelock, 27; quoted, 225

embryo, rudimentary organs of, 43–44

engagements. *See* betrothal customs

English language. *See* language

environment: and gender identity, 87–88, 120–121, 233; heredity vs., 37–38, 62, 78, 81; human adaptation to, 110, naturist theory and, 37. *See also* society

"Eonism," 25, 27 29

Ericsson, R. J., 43

eroticism: adolescent, 158, 164–167; children and, 134–136, 142; in elderly, 221 222; and erotic signals, 162–164; female, 162–164, 176; and fetishism, 216; male,

INDEX